CW00848340

Frank J. Gent

The Trial of the Bideford Witches

Crediton
MMXVII

Copyright © 2017 Frank J. Gent

The author has asserted their moral right under the Copyright, Designs and Patents Act, 1988, to be identified as the author of this work.

All Rights reserved. No part of this publication may be reproduced, copied, stored in a retrieval system, or transmitted, in any form or by any means, without the prior written consent of the copyright holder, nor be otherwise circulated in any form of binding or cover other than that in which it is published and without a similar condition being imposed on the subsequent purchaser.

First published 1982.

New edition 1998. Updated 15th May, 1999.

New edition September, 2001.

New edition 2002.

This edition 2017.

Contents

A True and Impartial

RELATION

OF THE

INFORMATIONS

AGAINST

Three Witches,

Viz. {
TEMPERANCE LLOYD,
MARY TREMBLES, and
SUSANNA EDWARDS.
}

Who were Indicted, Arraigned, and Convicted
at the Assizes holden for the County of *DEVON*
at the Castle of *EXON, Aug.* 14. 1682.

WITH

Their several CONFESSIONS, taken before
Thomas Gist Mayor, and *John Davie* Alderman
of *Biddiford* in the said County, where
they were Inhabitants.

AS ALSO

Their SPEECHES, CONFESSIONS, and
BEHAVIOUR, at the time and place of Execution
on the Twenty fifth of the said Month.

LONDON:
Printed by *Freeman Collins*, and are to be Sold by *T. Benskin*, in
St. *Brides* Church-yard, and *C. Yeo* Bookseller in *Exon.* 1682.

A True and Impartial Relation... *(1682): the depositions in the cases against the Bideford witches*

Forewords

1982

The trial of the Bideford witches in 1682 although well-known has been little studied. Previous accounts have concentrated on reproducing the original sources mostly for their antiquarian and sensational value, and no attempt made to analyse and understand the events in their wider social and historical context.

The Bideford trial merits closer examination in several respects. Firstly, it came at the very end of the witch-hunting craze of 1550 to 1660. There were very few executions for witchcraft in England after the Restoration, and the Bideford witches were almost the last to be executed in England. By that time most witchcraft trials ended in acquittals; the circumstances in which such a retrogressive act could have taken place deserve careful study.

Secondly, the trial was exceptional in that it concerned events in an urban, even cosmopolitan, environment. Most studies of seventeenth-century witchcraft concentrate on village life; how did it occur in a thriving, bustling provincial town with a cultured, educated and wealthy elite? A third problem which needs to be studied is the apparent acquiescence of the victims in their fate. They appear to have made little or no attempt to deny the charges made against them either before or during their trial.

Finally, the trial gives us an extraordinary, exceptional and valuable insight into the lives and mentality of ordinary people at the close of the seventeenth century. We hear the very words they spoke, we can recapture the excitement of those distant events in a way no other source could provide.

1998

When I originally wrote this booklet, already fifteen years ago, I was living in Bideford without any income as I renovated an old cottage. Access to major libraries was difficult, for reasons of distance as well as finance. I did not read, for instance, Wallace Notestein's *History of Witchcraft in England*. I finally read a copy a year ago, and was impressed with his work, well in advance of his time. He gives a very good account of Joseph Glanville's work, corroborating what I also felt. He also had access to another pamphlet about these trials, published in 1687. I went to the trouble of seeing a copy of his book after reading Antonia Fraser's *The Weaker Vessel*, where she recounts the story of the Bideford Witches using Notestein as her source. Although her account of the trial is not very clear, the book as a whole provides an excellent background to the topic and period.

My own booklet received a kind review in *Devon & Cornwall Notes & Queries* after I published it, and I quickly sold enough copies to recover my expenses. Since then it had been forgotten, but once it was footnoted in the book *Wenches, Wantons and Witches* by Marianne Hester it began to be noticed and there has been a renewed interest. The National Curriculum has also led to some interest from schools.

For the past few years I have worked from an office next to the courts in Exeter, the old Assizes where the witches were tried and sentenced. I was surprised and moved when I came back from my summer holiday in September 1996 to look out of my office window and see a new plaque affixed to the wall of Rougemont Castle bearing the following inscription:

THE DEVON WITCHES
IN MEMORY OF
Temperance Lloyd
Susannah Edwards
Mary Trembles
OF BIDEFORD DIED 1682
Alice Molland
DIED 1685
THE LAST PEOPLE IN ENGLAND
TO BE EXECUTED FOR WITCHCRAFT
TRIED HERE & HANGED AT HEAVITREE
In the hope of an end to persecution & intolerance

Almost certainly, though, the Bideford women were the last to be executed for witchcraft in England. The only evidence for this dubious honour belonging to Alice Molland (or Welland) comes from *Side-lights on the Stuarts* by J. Inderwick. According to his extracts from the Gaol Books, which do not appear to have been checked by subsequent scholars, she was found guilty of witchcraft and sentenced by Chief Baron Montagu, and left for execution. It would appear that execution never took place, for nothing survives in the form of the ballads and broadsides that marked any public executions.

2002

It is twenty years since Frank Gent's *The Trial of the Bideford Witches* was first published. It was a timely publication that appeared on the tercentenary of the events that culminated in the execution of Temperance Lloyd, Susanna Edwards and Mary Trembles in Exeter, 1682. It is fortunate that this classic local study of the dynamics of witch prosecution in a small community will be made available to a new audience. Not only to assist in the invaluable task of bringing into the corpus of historical memory the misdeeds of the past, but to emphasise that within specific contexts such actions are capable of being carried out in any period, including our own. Such an account offers a useful corrective to the impression of witchcraft and the prosecution of its supposed practitioners as simply being a remnant of the past.

What Gent so effectively demonstrates is the powder keg of loyalties and allegiances that underpinned life in Restoration Bideford—the fierce competitiveness both locally (with Barnstaple) and internationally arising out of mercantile trade was part of this. It is an important reminder that Bideford was once an important part of a burgeoning transatlantic trading network that laid the foundations for modern imperial and industrial Britain. The investigation of the violent acts of exclusion that lie at the centre of the Bideford witches, touches not just a small port on the north Devonian coast, but also the lives and concerns of those that sailed to Ireland, France, Spain, Newfoundland, New England, Virginia and Barbados. Family networks criss-crossed the ocean. The vehemence of local attacks on dissenters, (for a while excluded from political power in the borough) was pitched alongside the influx of outsiders seeking fortune in a booming port. The pressure on the resources of the community this created is so vividly captured by Gent in the concerns surrounding public health over dirt and disease. The identity of the town, its disparate social links and networks, the expansion and restructuring which must have turned the place into a permanent building site, the large numbers of strangers passing through or staying, the general flux in populations, all contributed to the unstable foundations of the port. Economic demands for labour were at odds with the social requirements of an orderly community. The close proximity of many people placed immense strain on resources and communal bonds. The prevailing sense of ambiguity in authority, (political, ecclesiastical) exacerbated the sense of uncertainty. Witchcraft needs to be seen as an expression of a soured, rancorous exchange, the outgrowth of a deadly and poisoned relationship. In a town considered in constant danger from disease, the extent of dissent (religious and drunken) heightened the lack of protection. The corrupted exchange, which lies at the core of witchcraft, could thrive in a community that experienced little in the sense of firm boundaries and reliable safeguards. The trial of the Bideford witches constitutes something of a sea change in events of the period. Identified by many (following Lord North's comments at the trial in Exeter) as signifying the growing disbelief amongst the prosecuting authorities in the validity of the charge of *maleficium*. The 1680s also witness the emergence of a new form of order to the town of Bideford itself, the quieter, wealthier and attractive place that Daniel Defoe described in the 1720s. Gent's book captures the competing elements that led to the formation of that more orderly community, as well as bringing voice and immediacy to the seemingly chaotic events of the initial interrogation of the three unfortunate women.

I hope that the re-publication of this book inspires others to explore the many links between the history of a local community and the wider world. It certainly inspired me to delve deeper into the culture and beliefs of the period. Whether it be in terms of popular beliefs, political conflicts, religious disputes, economic ties or the movements and histories of families once associated with the fortunes of this distinctive community, this is a book that speaks for all. Since the publication of the book in 1982, a plaque has appeared in Exeter to commemorate the lives of the three witches. It would be timely indeed if that act of acknowledgement of the weight of history could also be extended to the town where the women were initially accused, and where they lived.

Kevin Stagg
Cardiff, University of Wales
October 2002

2017

This book was republished in a fine edition in 2002 by Edward Gaskell of Bideford. That edition has now sold out. As I reach the end of my life I should like to make sure that the book remains available for a little longer.

I need to inform new readers that there are twenty-three clips by Michael Noonan of me talking about the Bideford witchcraft trials available on YouTube, under the heading 'Devon Witches Frank Gent'. In addition, I had the pleasure of meeting a couple of years ago B. Chris Nash, a native of Bideford and now of Ontario in Canada, author of *Temperance Lloyd; Hanged for Witchcraft in 1682*. This is a fictionalised account of the Bideford witchcraft case.

Frank Gent
Crediton
March 2017

Chapter 1
Seventeenth-century Bideford

Bideford at the end of the seventeenth century was a prosperous port, a pioneer in the trade with Newfoundland and Virginia that grew up as a consequence of its connection with the Grenville family. Sir Richard Grenville, the Elizabethan explorer, was 'determined to infuse new life into the town, something of his own energetic spirit.'[1] In 1573 Grenville gave Bideford a charter of incorporation, establishing self-government with a mayor and burgesses, which set it firmly on the path to success. He made one of his homes there, overlooking the quay, and it was from Bideford that he set out for many of his voyages, and many of his crew were natives of the town.[2]

It was as a consequence of these voyages that Bideford developed its important trade in tobacco from the colony of Virginia. By the 1720s eight and a half million pounds of tobacco were landed annually on Bideford Quay, most of which was re-exported by way of Amsterdam to the rest of Europe.

The trade in coal was increasing; the small, local supply formerly mined in the town was replaced as the seam was exhausted with imports from South Wales, and was used by industries such as brewing, malt making, lime burning and smithing for which local timber supplies were no longer adequate.

The wool trade was also important, and had started as long ago as the fifteenth century, arriving at the port from Spain and proceeding thence to Tiverton. It was transported by packhorse, crossing over the then narrow bridge and helping to pay for its reconstruction in stone in the early sixteenth century, thereby substantiating the tradition that Bideford bridge was built on wool—or at least on the profits that it brought to the town.[3] It was a cargo of Spanish wool that was unfairly blamed for bringing plague to Bideford in 1646. The trade from Spain was gradually supplanted during the seventeenth century by a supply from Ireland, most of which came to England through Bideford.

Bideford was the most important port in Devon for the trade with Newfoundland. The Bideford ships went out each year across the Atlantic to catch and cure fish. At the end of the season they brought their catch back and sold it chiefly to the countries of southern Europe.[4]

Bideford reached its economic zenith during the period 1680 to 1720. But as the connection with the American colonies was the source of its wealth, so was it the cause of Bideford's decline in the mid-eighteenth century as those colonies fought for and gained their independence. It was not until the nineteenth century that the decline was halted and Bideford regained some of its former prestige.

The government of Bideford at that time consisted of a mayor, four aldermen and ten capital burgesses, together with a recorder, a town clerk, two sergeants at mace and various other officers. These rights, confirmed and extended by the charters issued by James I in 1610 and 1619, were based on those obtained by Sir Richard Grenville from Queen Elizabeth I in 1573 which made the town a free borough.[5] The capital burgesses correspond to modern councillors, except that they were not elected but were a self-appointed and self-perpetuating oligarchy, consisting of the wealthiest families of the town, closely linked with each other by business and by marriage. When for example in 1674 the council subscribed their names to a letter they were ten in number, and eight of that number held office as mayor during the period 1662 to 1676.[6] Furthermore, all of these men, unless prevented from doing so by death, held the office again, some on three or even more occasions. This same pattern continued throughout the next century, power being retained in the hands of this powerful minority.

The merchant class was often recruited from outside Bideford, mostly from the surrounding parishes of North Devon, but also from further afield. One of the latter was William Ernle who made his will in July 1662 and who was buried on 23 March 1663. He was a bachelor, and left all his belongings to his kinsmen, chiefly in Wiltshire, his county of origin. He was one of the stern-faced puritans, bequeathing his 'best bible of Geneva print' to John Ernle of Newburgh in Yorkshire. He had purchased property in the Bideford area, and owned other property in Somerset and Wiltshire. He left monetary bequests totalling £196—a sizeable sum.[7]

Overmantel formerly in the townhouse of Sir Beville Grenville, Bideford

It is clear from the few wills that have survived for the period 1663 to 1693 that the merchants' wealth was founded on the overseas trade. William Greening made his will in August 1671 not long before his death, and in his father's lifetime. He left all his goods to his wife and son, who was also his namesake. Most of his wealth was invested in ships, of which he shared ownership together with other Bideford merchants. He owned several houses in Bideford and land and other buildings in Abbotsham and Buckland Brewer, not far from the town. He left small bequests to his servant and his apprentice. As was the custom, he left five pounds to be handed out amongst the poor of Bideford at his funeral. He appointed his brothers John and Richard as his executors.[8]

Richard Greening made his own will in June 1677, though it was not proved until after his death in 1686. Like his brother William he described himself as a mariner. He owned a house at Filleigh, near South Molton, which he gave to his wife. To his son John he gave his lands in Okehampton together with a house in Appledore. His son Richard received 'the house upon the quay of Bideford wherein I now dwell.' He

3

was anxious to provide for his children, leaving them cash bequests totalling £400, and a dowry for his daughter Elizabeth of £200. He left five shillings to each of his brothers and sisters 'in remembrance of my love to them and that I was their brother.'[9]

John Darracott described himself as a merchant in his will dated 13 April 1672, two months before his death. He was one of the large and important Darracott clan, leaving property 'together with all my ships and parts of ships in Bideford and also in Ilfracombe and Combe Martin' to his wife Dorothy, his three sons John, Samuel and Daniel, and his daughter Sarah. He also gave his wife his 'dwelling house in Bideford called the brewhouse together with the furnace, brewing vats and vessels.' It seems he was a brewer as well as a merchant.[10]

When Henry Amory, mariner, made his will in August 1686, nearly two years before his death, he itemised forty bequests to his family and relations, and also bequeathed 'to John Bartlett's four daughters and son five pounds each.' This makes it clear that he was a member of the Nonconformist congregation of Bideford, as does the bequest of six pounds to Jonathan Bowden, for he and John Bartlett were respectively teacher and minister of the Great Meeting in Bideford. He had no children of his own, and left much of his wealth to Thomas Chope, 'son of my brother-in-law.' This included a half of the ship *Diamond* 'and with what doth to her belong', his rights in the ship *Ruby*, also property in Monkleigh and Weare Giffard, just outside Bideford, and a life interest in Henry Amory's house in Bideford. He also owned a quarter share in a 'bark called *Rosmerche*' which he gave to another cousin. His 'beloved wife Grace Amory' he appointed executor of his will, 'to whom I give what I have both at sea and shore.'[11]

John Frost was mayor of Bideford in 1666 and 1675. He made his will in June 1686 and was buried on 4 November 1687. He was by then a widower, and a successful merchant. His daughter Sarah had married Daniel Darracott, son of the John who made his will in 1672. His other daughter Hester was married to Richard Smith, an Exeter merchant. To their children, John and Daniel Darracott and Mary Smith, he left all his property in Allhalland Street, Bideford, together with £100 in cash to John and Mary, and £50 to Daniel. John Frost too had acquired properties outside Bideford, which he also gave to his daughters.[12]

Hartwell Buck made his will in May 1691, and was buried the following October. His family had to come to Bideford from Ireland, making their fortune in the wool trade, and rising to prominence in the town. His son became mayor in 1693, first of many of the family to hold the office. In his will, after the usual bequests to the poor and his maid servant, he left legacies of fifty shillings each to 'Mr James Wood our pastor' and to 'Jonathan Bowden our teacher'—the Bucks were leading Nonconformists in Bideford. He too had acquired country property, but most of his wealth was in shipping. His son John received the house; to his other son, George, he gave 'when it is received £100, part of a greater sum due from Their Majesties for my ship's hire.' His vessel had been commandeered for use in the war against France waged by William of Orange from 1688 to 1697. George also received 'one eighth part of my ship Happy Returns with what shall belong to her right that time.'[13]

George Darracott, of the same family as John, at his death in July 1693 left bequests totalling the remarkable sum of £950 in cash to his sons William, James and Charles, in addition to houses and lands in Bideford. Two of his sons were minors at his death and he did 'desire my brother-in-laws Mr John Darracott and Mr Thomas Hamett and also my sister Sarah Hamett and my good friend Mr William Mill to see that my will to be performed as near they can and that my said children be brought in learning and in the fear of the Lord taking the care and government of them until twenty-one.' He, like so many, was fearful of leaving his orphan children to fend for themselves and preserve their inheritance in a predatory world.[14]

Abraham Gearing made his will on his deathbed in 1693. This will too shows the close links that existed between the members of the merchant class. He appointed 'Daniel Darracott, John Smith and Thomas Chope the younger all of Bideford aforesaid merchants' as overseers of his will, giving them forty shillings each to purchase mourning rings. All three of them appeared in earlier wills as legatees. To his widowed mother Joan Gearing he left 'my featherbed performed in the dining room.' To his wife he left £200, and to his daughters Sarah and Hannah he left the enormous sum of £600 each as dowries. He too was a Nonconformist, leaving £5 to the Reverend James Wood 'to preach my funeral sermon.' He remembered his maidservant with twenty shillings. He ended his will: 'And my mind will have intent and meaning in that if it shall please God that the child which my said wife is now good with be a son then I do ordain such son to be the executor.'[15]

Christopher Pollard was a son of Bideford who made his fortune in the Newfoundland trade, describing himself in his will as 'an inhabitant of Caplin Bay in the Newfoundland, gentleman.' In 1699 there were twenty eight ships and 146 boats from Bideford engaged in the Newfoundland trade, ranging in size from 220 tons with sixty-five men and twenty guns, to sixty tons, twenty men and no guns.[16] Christopher Pollard was owner of one of the latter: he left to his son John his ship 'the Terrenovy Merchant of the burthen of eighty tons and all fittings' . His two other sons, Christopher and George, received only ten shillings each, while he bequeathed to 'my trusty and well-beloved wife Ann Pollard £100.' As for his four daughters, Ann Baker was already a widow, and received £50. He left the same amount to another daughter, 'Ellinor wife of John Lile in Newfoundland.' His daughters Mary and Joan were married to two mariners of Northam, William Bennett and George Handford, and they received ten pounds apiece.[17]

Thomas Conybeare was another mariner who died in 1692. He had inherited lands at Stowford in Swimbridge from his father George and his brothers Lewis and Peter. These lands he now left to his wife; her father and his brother were appointed 'rulers in trust to see that my wife and children be not wronged.' His son Edward and daughter Mary received £20 each.[18]

Mary Beard was buried on 31 January 1693.[19] She had no wealth or property to dispose of, but she was proud of her clothes, which she valued sufficiently to give her friends at her death. To her sister Phoebe she gave 'a black silk scarf and hat, a gold ring and a pair of gloves.' Her other sister Sarah received a gold ring. To 'Mary Frye that lived with me' she gave 'three suits of my headcloths and my black gown and my striped petticoat . ' She gave the remainder of her wardrobe to her stepmother, and the rest of her belongings she asked to be shared between her stepmother and her 'dear friend Henry Paul of Bideford, mason.' These were her deathbed wishes and Henry no doubt was her love. She, with so many others, was a victim of the small pox epidemics that raged with such virulence at that time.[20]

POPULATION

	Total Births	Total Deaths	Estimated Population
1600-09	359	276	1077
1610-19	395	207	1185
1620-29	444	215	1665
1630-39	582	413	1746
1640-49	593	729	1779
1650-59	583	372	1749
1660-69	589	635	1767
1670-79	640	630	1920
1680-89	870	937	2610
1690-99	656	955	1968
1700-09	638	789	1914

Population of Bideford 1600–1709

We can see quite clearly from this table how the population of Bideford was growing during the seventeenth century. The estimates for the population are based on the average annual baptisms for each ten-year period.[21] There was rapid growth during the decade 1620–9, when the population increased by more than fifty per cent. It then remained stable around the 1,750 mark for the next forty years until the 1680s when Bideford's fortunes began their meteoric rise which was to last for the next half century, and the population reached about 2,600. The registers show a decrease in baptisms after the 1680s which reflects the importance of Nonconformity in the town.

Most of the increase in the size of the population was due to the immigration of people from Bideford's agricultural hinterland who were attracted by Bideford's prosperity. They came also from elsewhere in Devon, from across the Bristol Channel, as the many names of Welsh origin testify, including the spouses of two of the witches. People also came from Ireland, as a consequence of the wool trade, including the Buck family which rapidly rose to prominence in the town. Others came from Scotland, and many came as refugees from France after 1685 to form Bideford's Huguenot community which survived until the mid-eighteenth century.

The burials recorded in the parish registers also reflect the growth of the population—the annual entries more than trebled between the beginning and end of the century—and also show the years of exceptionally high mortality which occurred in 1604, 1629, 1635, 1643 and 1646. 1646 was the year of the outbreak of plague in Bideford in which well over two hundred people lost their lives, though the outbreak in the summer of 1643 was almost as serious. At the end of the century there were similarly years of high mortality in 1680, 1689, 1690 and 1696, as a result of smallpox epidemics. Over three hundred people died in the 1689–90 outbreak.[22] It is clear from the parish registers that Bideford in the 1680s must have been an extremely crowded town, coping with a huge increase in its population, and in conditions which would be conducive to outbreaks of disease. This evidence is supported by the records of the town, with frequent attempts to improve sanitation and hygiene, and including, for example the provision of tobacco barrels as dustbins.[23]

POVERTY

The growth of the population brought with it the problem of poverty, and the many charities founded during the seventeenth century to assist the poor of Bideford are a reflection of the concern shown. John Strange, mayor and 'saviour' of Bideford during the outbreak of plague in 1646, in which he himself died, left money in his will for the erection of five almshouses in Meddon Street for the use of 'poor old people' Amory's almshouses in Old Town were founded in 1663 providing homes for six old people. Baron's charity of 1681 was intended for the 'relief of poor seamen and their widows.'[24] The great increase in the size of the population placed a strain on the town's resources for dealing with the poor. The ruling oligarchy, here as elsewhere at the time, was anxious to avoid the burden of high poor rates and to this end took various measures: restricting the admission of new people to the town, and obtaining assurances from the fathers of girls who bore illegitimate children that they would take financial responsibility for their grandchild.[25] This resistance to the obligation of dealing with the problem of the poor was especially acute in a community where most people lacked roots, where the extended family and bond of neighbourliness in village life were not available to provide support. In the change from a rural to an urban society 'neighbours in a community were ceasing to practise mutual help; resentment, jealousy and suspicion gave rise to accusations. Proceeding from this interesting explanation, it is possible to argue that the victimisation of the lower classes, of the poor and unfortunate, was also the result of a change in the structure of community relations.'[26] The class of 'victims' can be further narrowed: 'the overwhelming majority of alleged witches were women, usually old women. By the logic of this a large proportion were widows.'[27]

8

POLITICS AND RELIGION

The reign of Charles II was a time of exceptional political upheaval, particularly the 1680s. The supposed Popish Plot of 1679 was succeeded by many other threatened risings, one of the most serious occurring in 1683 with the Rye House Plot. These periods of political uncertainty culminated in Monmouth's rebellion of 1685, after the death of Charles II, his natural father, and the flight of Monmouth's uncle James II in 1688. The handling of the trials that followed each of these events earned the Stuart judiciary an unsavoury reputation. Many were condemned on the flimsiest of evidence, making a mockery of justice.

After the restoration of the monarchy in 1660 Nonconformists were persecuted and oppressed under the terms of the 'Clarendon Code': the tables were turned and they were made to suffer the same disabilities as they had applied to the Anglican church. The change had considerable impact in Bideford where there was a large Nonconformist congregation. The Presbyterian minister of Bideford, William Bartlett, was removed from the parish church in 1662; he became minister of the Nonconformist congregation that exists to this day, and died in 1682. One of his successors at the parish church was Nathaniel Eaton, formerly a leading Presbyterian, and first president of Harvard College in America, but 'he conformed to the ceremonies of the Church of England, and was fixed in this very town of Bideford, where he became a bitter persecutor of those who kept faithful to that way of worship which he himself had quitted.'[28] He came to Bideford in 1668, but died, deeply in debt, in the King's Bench prison at Southwark in 1674.[29] One of the political consequences of the religious changes was that Nonconformists were excluded for a while from the government of Bideford, which remained in the hands of a small conforming minority. This Anglican oligarchy filled the offices of the corporation. This is well illustrated by the action taken by the mayor against the Nonconformists. On 19 June 1670 John Bartlett, a renowned Nonconformist and formerly rector of St Mary Major's in Exeter, was arrested at the house of Sarah Dennis by the constables and churchwarden. They were fined £20 each and the members of the congregation were fined five shillings. [30]

The town clerk of Bideford, John Hill, was one of the new men, aggressive in his support of the king and the Anglican settlement, virulent in his persecution of the Nonconformists. The Conventicle Act of 1664, part of the 'Clarendon Code', outlawed religious services other than those of the church of England, at whose services attendance was mandatory, under pain of fines, such as were imposed at Bideford. In a letter written on 6 December 1670 John Hill wrote:

As touching the Northam fanatics, I am glad they are at last convinced of their errors. Well fare the coercive power over them. I am afraid that they more fear the rod than him that holds it, just like a few of them in this town, who have been long settled on their lees, and being lately whipped out of their lazy condition, feeling the smart of the penalty some comply. But others remain obstinate, against whom I am providing a scorpion according to the statute.[31]

This 'scorpion' took the form of a raid on 15 April 1671 on a service taking place at the house of Samuel Johns, where over forty people were found and charged. Johns was fined £20 plus £10 towards the fine of the preacher who had fled evading capture. The congregants were fined from £2 to £5 each, plus five shillings each towards the fine of the nonconforming minister.[32]

On Sunday, 17 May 1674 about four hundred people, mostly of Bideford, attended a Nonconformist service at the house of Gabriel Beale, to the considerable consternation of the mayor and council.[33] The Religious Census held in 1674 recorded that there were ninety-six Nonconformists in Bideford and a similar number in neighbouring Northam,[34] but these figures seem very low when compared with the estimate of four hundred persons attending the service given by Mr Bartlett.[35] This represented perhaps one quarter of the total population of the town, and it is no surprise that the authorities were initially at a loss how to proceed in the face of such large scale disregard of the Act. John Hill estimated the figure even higher. He wrote on 2 July 1672 '...a great barn and shippen is in finishing for the fanatics' preacher, whereto more than a third part of this town do contribute largely.'[36] The exclusion of such a large number of people from the official government of the town was one cause of the resentment and lack of respect with which the corporation had to contend. A further raid under the terms of the Conventicles Act took place on the house of Gabriel Beale on 26 April 1685.[37] The political situation continued to be unstable, and several Nonconformists left Bideford to join Monmouth's rebellion in June and July 1685—some of them were subsequently captured and executed at the Bloody Assizes, and their quartered bodies returned to their home town to discourage further trouble.[38] The situation was eventually resolved by the removal of many of the restrictions after the accession of William of Orange in 1688. Nonconformists returned to take their place in the government of the town, so much so that by 1720 'the corporation consisted for the most part of dissenters.'[39]

VIOLENCE

Violence was an accepted and normal part of seventeenth century life. At the national level, during the civil war, it had affected the whole of society, in skirmishes and battles, the execution of the king and locally in the accidental death of two hundred Royalist prisoners when their secret arsenal exploded in Torrington church, and the many burials of soldiers recorded in the parish register of Bideford.

The decade 1675 to 1685 was particularly marked by the problems of internal disorder in the town, a consequence of the religious and political strife. The mayor and one of the aldermen of Bideford were ex officio justices of the peace, a power that was a cause of resentment. There was official disapproval of drinking and gambling, there being many alehouses, a large number of which were unlicensed. Those licensed numbered thirty-four in 1674, increasing to fifty-eight by 1687.[40] Society seems to have been polarised between puritans and tipplers, and the latter problem affected all levels. We can follow the progress of Richard Allen through the records as an example. He was a bricklayer, one of the new trades in Bideford at that time that developed to build the new homes of the prosperous merchants. On 9 September 1675 he was brought before the mayor and town clerk and fined for swearing more than five hundred 'profane oaths'. He attempted to restrain his tongue, though he let slip one more oath a fortnight later for which he received a further fine. Two years later he was involved in a brawl in the town. Whilst at the George Inn he lent a club to the servant of George Carey, squire of Clovelly, for the servant to use in a fight in the buttgarden. In April 1678 he was bound over by the justices for 'abusing Michael Ogilby the rector on Sunday in church'.

The example of Richard Allen can be seen higher up the social ladder in no less a person than this same rector that he had abused. Michael Ogilby was appointed to Bideford in 1674, to succeed Nathaniel Eaton, and his presence was a constant source of friction in the town. In February 1676 he came to the mayor in fear of his life, 'having causes and apprehensions of fear best known to God and himself and did take his corporal oath that George Cole esquire of Bideford and Anne his wife would beat wound, maim or kill him or procure some others to do him some bodily harm.' At this stage the mayor acted with caution, expecting the affair to blow over and the parties to make their peace, but in this he was disappointed for 'on the next day, Mr Ogilby being abused by Sir John Stonehouse, Mr Cole's son-in-law, and threatened to have his head cloven, repaired to me the town clerk with Mr Mayor (I the town clerk being then lame with gout).' The mayor took limited action: 'One of the constables only, went in a civil manner and acquainted Sir John and Mr Cole herewith, who in most vilifying manner reproached the mayor, girt their swords, bid defiance and come at their perils etc.'40 What is remarkable is their quickness to anger, regardless of social class, and their contempt of authority in the persons of the mayor and the rector. The townspeople of Bideford showed consistently that they had little respect for the nominal leaders of their society.

To return to the brawl in the buttgarden mentioned earlier, the main contender was John Collacott of Alwington, described, though not behaving, as a gentleman. The subject of the quarrel is unrecorded, but earlier the same day he had been fined one shilling for 'swearing of one profane oath' in the mayor's presence. That evening he was fighting with Roger Mayne of Parkham and others. George Carey's servant got the club from Richard Allen with the intention that 'he would knock Roger Mayne down as he went into the higher part of the buttgarden.'40

In 1680 Richard Sleeper, a freeman of Bideford, a locksmith and also the licensee of the Blacksmiths' Arms fell foul of mayoral power after he 'declared many contemptuous words and unbeseeming language of the chief magistrate of this town in very contumelious manner... when... the common council of this borough were assembled in the guildhall.' He was made an example of, and was sent to 'His Majesty's prison in this town' and had his licence rescinded and the sign removed from his premises.

In February 1681 a notorious alehouse keeper, Peter Bagilhole, similarly used 'very abusive language of Mr Thomas Gist, mayor, and Mr John Hill, town clerk.' Thomas Gist appears to have been a most unpopular mayor. It was during his mayoralty that the trial of the witches took place, and he was responsible for the action taken against them. In August 1682, at the time of their execution, several depositions were made by one of the constables and two townsmen against Thomas Michelson, a Scot who had settled in the town, 'of his several misdemeanours towards Mr Thomas Gist, mayor.' His servant was also in trouble and had 'the peace sworn against him by Elizabeth Angell, for very abusive language used to her on the bridge, and for throwing of her hat over out in the river.'40

The many examples of disrespect for the office of mayor and chief magistrate continue. In January 1683 several people made statements 'against William Jones, one of the tide waiters [dockers] belonging to the port of Bideford, concerning his abuses done against Mr Mayor and some other officers of the corporation. Upon his refusal to find bail he was committed to prison from whence he escaped.' This prison was the old chapel at the west end of the bridge given to the corporation in 1575 by Sir Richard Grenville to act as the town lock-up.

In 1680 the rector, Michael Ogilby, was himself denounced by his indignant parishioners.[41] The complaints were numerous, and give us an insight into the mentality of a powerful minority of the people of Bideford at that time. The first complaint was on religious grounds:

> In the first place therefore we the jurors upon our oaths do present that Michael Ogilby upon Sunday the tenth day of October last past, and upon several Sundays and other times before, did permit and suffer one Mr Hann the younger to preach and to administer the holy communion in the parish church, and one Mr Hann the elder to preach and officiate in the same church to the respective congregations then assembled, Mr Hann and his son being at such times excommunicated persons or otherwise prohibited, Mr Ogilby at the time of Mr Hann the younger's administering the sacrament sitting in a chair which was placed on the north side of the communion table in the chancel of the church.

Mr Hann the elder was to figure prominently later in the lives of the witches at their executions.

An earlier complaint was that on 28 September 1679 'in the parish church while the congregation were there assembled in the time of divine service Mr Ogilby in most irreverent manner did rail and vilify one Robert Waycutt, yeoman, to the great grief of the people.' The list added that on 8 October 1679 'in the parish church as Mr John Hill, town clerk, was going out of the church after morning prayer, he did rail and bestow very much railing and unchristian language upon him, holding out of his staff, threatening and assaulting of him therewith.' It was also recorded that he had been heard to say that 'he could find it in his heart to kill' Simon Crymes, the bishop's surrogate, who was attempting to solve the religious problems in Bideford by persuading Mr Ogilby to take a curate. The final charge against him was 'being a very great drinker and immoderate lover of wine and strong drink, even to ebriety, and also... hath been very many times guilty of profane and dreadful swearing.'

The attempt to remove or curb him proved unsuccessful, and his bad behaviour continued. In May 1682 there was 'a great disturbance in the parish church between Mr Ogilby and Samuel Jones, Christopher Prust and Bennett Dunscomb.'[42] It was at this time that some of the women of the town began to suffer from the illnesses that were attributed to witchcraft.

On 11 November 1685 there were renewed complaints against the rector 'concerning his abusing and striking of Mr Mayor.' The two chief personages of the town had come to blows: some indication of the friction in society in Bideford at that time. It was against this backcloth of violence, struggle for authority and petty quarrelling that the trial of the three witches took place.

The earliest case of witchcraft in Bideford for which any record has survived occurred in 1658. Grace Ellyott was accused of witchcraft and sent by the justices to stand trial at the Exeter assizes. In the Bail Book it was recorded how she was dealt with: 'Josias Ellyott of Bideford, mercer, and Richard Wann of Great Torrington, tailor. That Grace Ellyott, wife of the aforesaid Josias Ellyott do appear next [assizes] and be of the good behaviour on suspicion of witchcraft. Appeared and discharged. Surety in twenty pounds apiece.'[43]

One of the people accused of witchcraft at the Exeter assizes in 1671 was Temperance Lloyd of Bideford. This was her first appearance, accused of 'killing William Herbert by witchcraft' but on this occasion she was acquitted. On 15 May 1679 'Temperance Lloyd was accused for practising of witchcraft upon Anne Fellow the daughter of Edward Fellow, of Bideford gentleman (Gauger of Excise). Evidences against her were: Anne Fellow the mother, Mr Oliver Ball apothecary, Elizabeth Coleman, Dorcas Lidston and Elizabeth Davie. Upon the 17 May 1679 the said Temperance was searched by Sisly Galsworthy and others.' The papers were filed, but no further action appears to have been taken.[44]

Chapter 2
The Justices' Enquiry

The lowest level for the administration of justice at that time consisted of the sessions of the peace which were operated by the justices. 'Justices of the peace for the counties derived their judicial authority from the commissions of the peace, which were issued to most of the knights and principal gentry and lawyers within each county.'[45] Bideford was separate from this system; under the terms of its charter granted by James I in 1610 it was empowered to hold its own sessions of the peace, with the mayor and one of the senior aldermen as ex officio justices of the peace for each year. These sessions were 'permanent', and could be convened at any time as required, unlike those for the county which met only on the four quarter days. Under the terms of the town's charter the Bideford justices were required and empowered 'to enquire... of all and every murders, felonies, witchcraft, incantations, sorceries, art, magic.'[46] It was with this authority that the Bideford magistrates acted when Temperance Lloyd was arrested on Saturday 1 July 1682. A prisoner had to be examined before a justice within three days, in the presence of the person who made the arrest and the accusers. If it appeared that a felony had been committed, then the prisoner could not be released, but the justices were to write down 'the examination of the said prisoner, and information of them that bring him, of the fact and circumstances thereof for certification to the next gaol delivery, which took place when the assize judges came on their twice-yearly circuit. The accusers were then bound over to appear and give evidence, and the suspect was either sent to gaol by mittimus or released on bail.[47] This was precisely the procedure followed at Bideford.

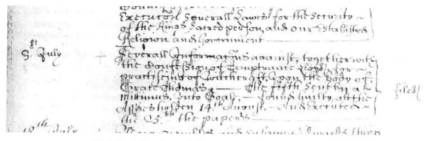

Bideford Sessions of the Peace Book, 3rd July, 1682

Temperance Lloyd

On Saturday 1 July 1682 Thomas Eastchurch, a Bideford shopkeeper, complained to some of the town's constables who then arrested Temperance Lloyd and locked her in the old chapel at the end of the bridge where she remained until taken before the justices on the Monday morning. The two justices that year were the mayor, Thomas Gist, and one of the aldermen, John Davie. Also present was the town clerk, John Hill, who recorded all the statements that were made. On that Monday statements were made by Thomas and Elizabeth Eastchurch, Grace Thomas, who was Elizabeth's sister and the alleged victim, and by their neighbours Anne Wakely and Honor Hooper. First of all the charges against Temperance Lloyd were read out, that *being brought before us by some constables of the borough upon the complaint of Thomas Eastchurch and charged upon suspicion of having used some magical art, sorcery or witchcraft upon the body of Grace Thomas and to have had discourse or familiarity with the devil in the likeness or shape of a black man.*[48] The reasons for this suspicion were recounted by Grace Thomas, who said *that upon or about the 30th day of September now last past she was going up the High Street of Bideford and she met with Temperance Lloyd who did then and there fall down on her knees to her, and wept, saying, 'Mistress Grace, I am glad to see you so strong again.' Upon which she replied, 'Why dost thou weep for me?' Unto which Temperance replied, 'I weep for joy to see you so well again.'* As she then pretended. Anne Wakely gave evidence *that she hath been an attendant of Grace Thomas about six weeks now last past; and that on Thursday... (which was the 29th of June) in the morning she did see something in the shape of magpie to come at the chamber window where Grace Thomas did lodge.'* This too was grounds for suspicion, and led her to question Temperance Lloyd who *was*

16

at that time down by Thomas Eastchurch's door. She continued in her evidence to give an account of how the previous day, Sunday 2 July, she *did search the body of Temperance Lloyd in the presence of Honor Hooper and several other women. And upon search of her body she did find in her secret parts two teats hanging nigh together like unto a piece of flesh that a child had sucked. And that each of the teak was about an inch in length.*

All the rest of the copious evidence against Temperance Lloyd was based on hearsay, usually of confessions which witnesses claimed to have overheard and then repeated to the justices without corroboration. No less than six of the statements in the trial were of this nature, those of Thomas Eastchurch and his wife, Anne Wakely, William Herbert William Edwards and Joan Jones. The first three belonged to the same household and presented the same story. William Herbert had a long-standing grievance based on his father's death bed accusation, and Joan Jones made her statement after her husband's epileptic attack before the justices. Some of their statements are so detailed and fanciful as to make us wonder at their motivation, plausibility and intent. Anne Wakely after seeing the magpie at the window claimed she *did demand of Temperance Lloyd whether she did know of any bird to come and flutter at the window. Unto which question Temperance did then say, that it was the black man in the shape of the bird.* Similarly, after finding the teats, she *did demand of her whether she had been sucked at that place by the black man (meaning the devil). Whereunto Temperance did acknowledge that she had been sucked there often times by the black man; and that the last time that she was sucked by the black man was the Friday before she was searched, which was the 30th day of June last past.*

The whole of Thomas Eastchurch's statement was based on what he claimed to have overheard Temperance Lloyd confess while she was in Bideford lock-up the previous day, Sunday. His evidence carried considerable weight, as a gentleman and respected citizen of the town: *The informant upon his oath saith, that upon yesterday, which was the second day of July, he did hear Temperance Lloyd to say and confess that about the thirtieth day of September last past, as she was returning from the bakehouse with a loaf of bread under her arm towards her own house, she did meet with something in the likeness of a black man in a street called Higher Gunstone Lane within this town, and then and there the black man did tempt and persuade her to go to his Thomas Eastchurch's house to torment Grace Thomas who is his sister-in-law. That Temperance did first refuse the temptation, saying that Grace Thomas had done her no harm. But afterwards by the further persuasion and temptation of the black man, she did go to his house, and that she went up the stairs after the black man, and confessed that both of them went into the chamber where his sister-in-*

law was, and there they found one Anne Wakely, rubbing one of the arms and one of the legs of Grace Thomas.

And he further saith that Temperance did also confess that the black man did persuade her to pinch Grace Thomas in the knees, arms and shoulders, intimating with her fingers how she did it. And that when she came down the stairs again into the street, she saw a braget [tabby] cat go into his shop, and that she believed it to be the devil.

And he did hear Temperance to say and confess that on Friday night last, which was the thirtieth day of June, the black man did meet with her near her own door about ten o' clock of that same night and there did again tempt her to go to his house and to make an end of Grace Thomas. Whereupon Temperance did go to his house with the black man and that she went into the chamber where Grace Thomas lay, and further did confess that she did pinch and prick Grace Thomas again in several parts of her body, declaring with both of her hands how she did do it, and that thereupon Grace Thomas did cry out terribly. And confessed that the black man told her that she should make an end of Grace Thomas. And further she did confess that the black man did promise her that no one should discover her or see her.

And she also confessed that about twelve o' clock of the same night the black man did suck her in the street in her secret parts, she kneeling down to him. That he had blackish clothes, and was about the length of her arm, that he had broad eyes, and a mouth like a toad, and afterwards vanished clear away out of her sight.

This informant further saith, that he heard Temperance to confess that about the first day of June last past the black man was with her again, and told her that on that night she should make an end of Grace Thomas, and confess that she had that night griped Grace Thomas in her belly, stomach and breast and clipped her to the heart. And she did cry out pitifully. And Temperance was about the space of two hours tormenting of her. And that one Anne Wakely with several other women were then present in the chamber, but could not see her Temperance, and that the black man stood by her in the same room also.

This informant further saith, that he supposed that Grace Thomas in her sickness had been afficted through a distemper arising from a natural cause, did repair unto several physicians, but that she could never receive any benefit prescribed by them.

His wife, Grace's sister, then gave her evidence. She stated that upon the second day of this instant July Grace Thomas then lodging in her husband's house, and hearing of her to complain of great pricking pains in one of her knees, *she did see her knee and observed that she had nine places in her knee which had been pricked, and that every of the pricks were as though it had been the prick of a thorn.* This was sufficient to arouse the suspicion of image magic, so that the same day she *did demand of Temperance Lloyd whether she had any wax or clay in the form of picture whereby she had pricked and tormented Grace Thomas. Unto which Temperance made answer that she had no wax nor clay, but confessed that she had only a piece of leather which she had pricked nine times.* No further reference was made to this that day, but the following morning the Eastchurches and their supporters *were dissatisfied in some particulars concerning a piece of leather which Temperance had confessed of unto Elizabeth Eastchurch.* The justices gave their permission for them to take Temperance to be questioned by the rector, Michael Ogilby, in the parish church. She admitted to him every crime that was suggested to her, however fanciful, including the accusation that *on Friday was sevennight, which was the twenty-third day of June last past, she came into Thomas Eastchurch's shop in the form and shape of a cat, and fetched out of the shop a puppet or picture, commonly called a child's baby [i.e. doll], and that she carried it up into the chamber where Grace Thomas did lodge, and left it about the bed whereon she did lie.* Temperance Lloyd understood well the charge of image magic, and was at pains to deny that she practised it, and *would not confess that she had pricked any pins in the puppet or baby picture, although she were demanded particularly that question by Mr Ogilby.*

William Herbert was the last person to make a statement against Temperance Lloyd; his involvement with her went back over many years. On 2 February 1671 *he did hear his father William Herbert to declare on his deathbed that Temperance Lloyd… had bewitched him unto death.* The father requested that his son *with the rest of his relations, should view his father's body after his decease, and that by his body they should see what prints and marks Temperance Lloyd had made upon his body. His father did lay his blood to the charge of Temperance Lloyd and desired his son to see her apprehended for the same, but that she was acquitted.* This was the case that was referred to earlier.

William Herbert senior died in the February of 1671, and Temperance Lloyd must have been kept in the gaol at Exeter until her trial at Exeter Castle on 5 April 1671. She was accused of killing William Herbert by witchcraft, and other evidence was given against her. It was at this trial that Lydia Burman testified that *Temperance Lloyd had appeared to her in the shape of a red pig* and her death in May 1672 was blamed on Temperance Lloyd, though no charges were pressed at the time.

Temperance Lloyd was herself questioned by the justices on 3 July 1682 after the majority of the witnesses had completed their statements, and she admitted all the charges made against her. The following day William Herbert *went to the prison of Bideford where Temperance was and demanded of her whether she had done any bodily harm or hurt unto his late father, unto which she answered and said, 'Surely William I did kill thy father.'*

He did demand of her further, whether she had done any hurt or harm to Lydia Burman. Unto which she answered that she was the cause of her death.

He demanded of her why she had not confessed so much when she was in prison last time. She answered that her time was not expired for the devil had given her greater power and a longer time.

And he did hear her confess that she was the cause of the death of Anne Fellow... and also that she was the cause of the bewitching out of one of the eyes of Jane the wife of Simon Dallyn, mariner.

What William Herbert reported, Temperance Lloyd readily confessed to the justices. They went through Thomas Eastchurch's statement point by point and she admitted every accusation. During further questioning she admitted causing the other deaths. The question of image magic was also further pursued, and Temperance Lloyd *being further demanded again in what part of the house of Mr Eastchurch or in what part of the bed whereon Grace Thomas lay she left the puppet or baby picture... saith that she would not nor must not discover for if she did discover the same that the devil would tear her in pieces.*

A few days later, on Saturday 8 July, Temperance Lloyd was committed to the gaol at Exeter to await trial for witchcraft at the next assizes against Grace Thomas, and the statements made against her were filed for later use. At the actual trial she continued to maintain her guilt. It was only at her execution that she fully comprehended her situation, and fearful of death denied most of the charges that had been made against her though admitting to Mr Hann the clergyman and to the sheriff of the county that she had indeed hurt Grace Thomas *because the devil met me in the street, and bid me kill her, and because I would not he beat me about the head and back.* Even at the foot of the scaffold she did not completely lose her self-delusion.

Mary Trembles and Susanna Edwards

At the very moment that Temperance Lloyd was put in the Bideford lock-up, Grace Thomas's pains ceased to afflict her, but those of Grace Barnes took a turn for the worse. That Sunday, 16 July 1682, at ten o' clock in the morning, Grace Barnes was *again taken worse than before, insomuch as four men and women could hardly hold her.* During the commotion that surrounded her seizure, Mary Trembles happened to be passing the house. Agnes Whitefield, one of the neighbours restraining Grace Barnes, *hearing somebody out at the door, she did open the door, where she found one Mary Trembles standing with a white-pot in her hands, as though she had been going to the common bakehouse.* Whilst taking her Sunday meal to be cooked in the communal oven, a custom which survived into this century in parts of Europe, she dropped some of the food from her pot outside the house. The inference drawn was that this was a deceit practised to disguise the malevolent intent of her visit. Grace Barnes, despite the severity of her attack, on discovering who was outside accused Mary Trembles of being *one of them that did torment her, and that she was now come to put her out of her life.*

Bideford Sessions of the Peace Book, Memorandum

Just over a week after Temperance Lloyd was committed to gaol, on Tuesday 18 July 1682, Mary Trembles was denounced to the authorities of the town and consequently arrested, together with her companion Susanna Edwards. At the inquiry Grace Barnes's husband John was the first to speak, accusing Mary Trembles of hurting his wife by witchcraft. William Edwards then accused Susanna and Mary with quite impossible charges, based on his claim to have overheard a confession by Susanna. People came to see and question the two women while they were in the town lock-up, as they had Temperance Lloyd. One of Susanna's visitors was John Dunning of Torrington to whom she allegedly gave a full confession of her activities as a witch. Though he was never called upon to validate this, it was this supposed confession that Joan Jones claimed to have overheard and then reported to the justices. It was in these distressful circumstances that Mary Trembles blamed Susanna Edwards for her misfortunes. Susanna herself must have been quite overwhelmed by the experience: the arrest, imprisonment, questioning and general harassment by all and sundry must have left her confused and bewildered. During her own questioning that morning Anthony, Joan Jones's husband, who had been present with a great many others in the guildhall, had remarked how Susanna did nervously *gripe and twinkle her hands upon her own body.* He accused her, saying, *'Thou devil, thou art now tormenting some person or other.'* He claimed that her reply was, *'Well enough, I will fit thee.'* At this point he left the guildhall in Bideford with one of the constables to bring the sick Grace Barnes from her home to confront her tormentor and make her statement.

Upon their return, as they were carrying her up the steps *Susanna Edwards turned about and Anthony Jones was taken in a very sad condition as he was leading and supporting Grace Barnes up the stairs of the Town Hall before the mayor and justices insomuch that he cried out, 'Wife, I am now bewitched by this devil!' and forthwith leapt and capered like a madman, and fell ashaking, quivering and foaming, and lay there for the space of half an hour like a dying or dead man.*

After this dramatic demonstration of the witches' supposed powers Grace Barnes did not make her statement, but the two justices proceeded immediately with their examination of Mary Trembles, who made a full confession of everything suggested to her, and blamed Susanna Edwards for her initiation into witchcraft. This was followed by a similarly straightforward examination of Susanna Edwards who likewise confessed to a mass of fanciful charges, including that *she did prick and torment Dorcas Coleman.* The following day, Wednesday 19 July, Anthony Jones was sufficiently recovered from his fit to make his own statement, giving a report of the previous morning's dramatic events. Later that day Mary and Susanna were both searched for any suspicious marks on their bodies. Then they were sent to Exeter to join Temperance Lloyd whilst awaiting their trial.

Grace Barnes in her statement repeated the story and added that she had some suspicion of Susanna Edwards *because that she would oftentime repair unto her husband's house upon frivolous or no occasions at all.* In this particular case we have a clear illustration of the effects of the breakdown of traditional attitudes of neighbourly behaviour. In her confession Mary Trembles gave her own version of the events of the previous Easter Tuesday: *She did go about the town to beg some bread, and in her walk she did meet with Susanna Edwards, who asked her where she had been. Unto whom she*

answered that she had been about the town and had begged some meat but could
get none. Whereupon she together with Susanna Edwards did go to John
Barnes's house in hope that there they should have some meat. But he not being
within his house they could get no meat or bread being denied by Grace Barnes
and her servant who would not give them any meat.

There was good reason for their begging, and perhaps for the refusal:
1682 was a year of shortages. In the words of a Lancashire diarist: 'The
winter this year proved very scarce of fodder, straw being short and the
grass burnt up in summer, so that little hay was got. People were very
much straitened to keep their cattle alive, and many starved.'[49] Having
failed in their attempt to beg for food, the two women tried to beg a
farthing's worth of tobacco, which being also refused it seems they went
away discontented, and when Grace Barnes was taken ill that night, she
dealt with her guilty feelings by accusing them of witchcraft.

Most of the evidence against the two women came from the statements
of William Edwards and Joan Jones, who both claimed to be reporting
what they had overheard. William Edwards said that the previous day,
July 17, *he did hear Susanna Edwards to confess that the devil had carnal*
knowledge of her body, and that he had sucked her in her breast and in her secret
parts. And further saith that he did hear her say that she and Mary Trembles did
appear hand in hand invisible in John Barnes's house where Grace the wife of
John Barnes did lie in a very sad condition. And further saith that he did then
also hear Susanna to say that she and Mary Trembles were at that time come to
make an end of her.

Joan Jones went into even greater detail about the confession she had
heard earlier the same day in the presence of John Dunning. She claimed
she did hear him to demand of Susanna Edwards how and by what means she
became a witch. Unto which question she did answer that she did never confess
before now, but now she would. Her story was simple, how she was on a time out
gathering of wood, at which time she did see a gentleman to draw nigh unto her,
whereupon she was in good hopes to have a piece of money of him. When
questioned further about the episode later, she said that *about two years ago*
she did meet with a gentleman in a field called Parsonage Close and saith that
his apparel was all of black upon which she did hope to have a piece of money of
him, whereupon the gentleman drawing near unto her she did make a curchy or
curtsy unto him as she did use so to do unto gentlemen... [and he] did ask her if
she was a poor woman. Unto whom she answered that she was a poor woman,
and that thereupon... the gentleman did say unto her that if she would grant him
one request that she should neither want for meat, drink nor clothes. Whereupon

she did say unto the gentleman, 'In the name of God, what is it that I shall have?'
Upon which the gentleman vanished clear away from her.

Joan Jones, not content with repeating what she had overheard, added *that after John Dunning was gone she did hear Susanna Edwards confess that... she with Mary Trembles and by the help of the devil did prick and torment Grace the wife of John Barnes.* She also heard Susanna say *that the devil did oftentimes carry about her spirit.* She also heard her confess to torturing Dorcas Coleman, and that *she was sucked in her breast several times by the devil in the shape of a boy lying by her in her bed, and that it was very cold unto her. And further said that after she was sucked by him, the boy or devil had the carnal knowledge of her body four several times.* The reference to coldness was to a commonly held belief of the time.

Joan Jones also reported the quarrel between the two women: *she did hear Mary Trembles to say unto Susanna Edwards, 'O thou rogue I will now confess all, for 'tis thou that hast made me to be a witch, and thou art one thyself and my conscience must swear it.' Unto which Susanna replied unto Mary Trembles, 'I did not think that thou wouldst have been such a rogue to discover [reveal] it.'*

In her confession Mary gave more details: *about three years last past one Susanna Edwards did inform her that if she would do as she did, she should do very well. Whereupon she did yield unto Susanna Edwards and said that she would neither want for money, meat or clothes.* These were the same promises that Susanna was supposed to have received.

The other evidence against Mary Trembles was negligible. Her main guilt was of being an associate of Susanna Edwards, rather than for any offence she had committed herself.

In these circumstances it is possible to understand the resentment that may have existed between the two women. Susanna Edwards herself later blamed Temperance Lloyd, saying *she was the cause of her bringing to die; for she said when she was first brought to gaol, if that she was hanged, she would have me hanged too.* Public opinion also blamed Temperance Lloyd as 'the woman that has debauched the other two.'

There were other stories associated with their short stay in Exeter gaol. They were visited by Mr Hann, the clergyman, who asked them before their execution. *'Was not the devil there with Susan when I was once in the prison with you, and under her coats? The other told me that he was there, but is now fled.'* A similar tale is recounted in the other pamphlet version of the trial, which says 'They also asserted that the devil came with them to the prison door and there left them.'[50]

On Wednesday 26 July John Coleman, Dorcas Coleman and Thomas Bremincom made belated statements against Susanna Edwards, to add some further information that had been forgotten earlier. This was filed in the dossier along with the other statements to be used at the trial a few weeks later. Dorcas Coleman recalled being taken ill at the end of August 1680 while her husband was away at sea. In his absence his uncle, Thomas Bremincom, had hurried to fetch the doctor, George Beare, who examined the patient and diagnosed witchcraft, unable to admit any failing in his own medical knowledge. Susanna Edwards then called to visit, and Dorcas accused her of being her tormentor, and attempted to *fly in her face* but collapsed unable to see or hear. Dorcas was trying to scratch Susanna above the heart: a well-known antidote for witchcraft.

The following week Grace Barnes was finally able to make her statement in time to be used at the trial, mostly reiterating what her husband had already said. The last statement was made by William Herbert just before the trial started in Exeter, recounting the confession he claimed to have received whilst visiting Temperance Lloyd in Bideford prison.

This is the general outline of the events that took place in the early summer of 1682. The accusations made against the women were typical of those made at that time in other cases of witchcraft. Temperance Lloyd was accused of causing the deaths of several people over a period of twelve years, some of which she had already been tried and acquitted for. She was also accused of causing sickness and having familiars. Additional evidence was her faulty repetition of prayers, her alleged secret teats, and her spectacular transformation into a cat. She was adamant however that she had not practised image magic by sticking pins into a doll or wax model. Similar crimes were attributed to Mary Trembles. She cursed Grace Barnes after being refused food, she went invisibly into Grace's house, she had a teat for the devil to suck in her 'privy parts', and she had carnal knowledge of the devil who, it was claimed, came to her in the form of a lion. Susanna Edwards was accused of bewitching Dorcas Coleman, also of being invisible, of attempting to murder Grace Barnes, of causing fits, of allowing the devil to suck her breasts and 'secret parts' and of having carnal knowledge of the devil when he came to her in the form of a boy.

The witches' confessions make clear the important distinction that has to be made between the accusations made when they were initially denounced, which reflect more closely the nature of popular contemporary witchcraft beliefs, and the infinitely more fanciful 'confessions' that were extracted by the magistrates using careful questioning or downright bullying, or 'overheard' by such people as Thomas Eastchurch. [see p. 17] These latter were the educated members of society who were more influenced by the literature of the time. It is often apparent that many of the statements were strongly influenced by the questions the magistrates must have asked.

The nature of witchcraft: frontispiece to Joseph Glanvill's Saducismus Triumphatus
(1681)

Chapter 3
Witchcraft beliefs in the late Sevententh Century

Folklore still played a large part in the beliefs of ordinary seventeenth-century people. Temperance Lloyd described in some detail the *black man*: She *said he was about the length of her arm and that his eyes were very big, and that he hopped or leapt in the way before her*. Susanna Edwards related a similar tale in her confession: *about two years ago she did meet with a gentleman in a field called the Parsonage Close in the town of Bideford. And saith that his apparel was all of black*. This was interpreted by her accusers into an appearance of the devil. Susanna Edwards claimed in her final confession upon the scaffold that he was *a short black man*, similar to Temperance Lloyd's claim. These apparitions belong to the world of pixies and goblins rather than of witchcraft and diabolism: 'These beings were in their origin the little people of folklore, transformed by Christian theology into demons and hence acquiring sinister attributes.'[51] These demons, it was commonly believed, 'had intercourse with the witches, or sucked the blood of their mistresses through "witches teats".'[52] Temperance Lloyd *also confessed that the black man did suck her in her secret parts, she kneeling down to him but his sucking was with a great pain unto her*. In the case of Susanna Edwards *the devil had sucked her in her breast and in her secret parts*. This sucking was interpreted as being the way in which witches fed blood to the devil or their familiars, the devil placing on the witch's body for this purpose 'a piece of flesh from which he, in his own person or that of a familiar, might such the blood of a witch.'[53]

It is important that the women were denounced as witches in explicitly sexual terms. In the words of one writer, 'The most that can be said at present on the sexual aspect of the trials is that the mythology of witchcraft was at its height at a time when women were generally believed to be sexually more voracious than men; 'of women's unnatural, unsatiable lust', wrote the bachelor, Robert Burton, in 1621, 'what country, what village doth not complain.'[54] It is also important that the Bideford witches were women alone, a spinster and two widows, and they do not appear to have had any children who might have defended them or defined their role as women.

The stereotype witch is an independent adult woman who does not conform to the male idea of proper female behaviour. She is assertive; she does not require or give love (though she may enchant), she does not nurture men or children, nor care for the weak. She has the power of words—to defend herself or to curse. In addition she may have other, more mysterious powers which do not derive from the established order.[55]

They were particularly threatening to patriarchal power and male domination at a time when Bideford was dealing with a large increase in its population, and the problem of caring for the aged poor, particularly women. And this threat was responded to with accusations of witchcraft, in particular of unnatural sexuality, with the devil or familiars, in whatever form they chose. Unable to nurture their own children, they instead fed these monsters.

The evidence recorded for use at the trial provides some fascinating insights into the mentality of the ordinary people of Bideford in the late seventeenth century. The depositions that they made are a reflection of their secret fears that normally never found expression, but in the extraordinary circumstances of the witch trial were able to surface in acceptable form. Most important was the universality of belief in witchcraft and its manifestations. Everyone, accusers, accused, victims, magistrates, gentlemen and common folk, clergy, judges and the writers of pamphlets accepted the existence of witches and their powers. The only person to have doubted their powers was Sir Francis North, Lord Chief Justice and partner with Judge Raymond on the 1682 Summer assize circuit.

The most important belief in the power of magic was the acceptance of the ability of witches to harm others by the practice of image magic, as is indicated by the Eastchurches' accusations and Temperance Lloyd's denials. They were quite convinced that a piece of leather was being pricked by Temperance Lloyd to induce pains in her victim. The small doll found near Grace Thomas's bed was similarly believed to have magical uses. People also believed in the power of cursing: Grace Barnes turned away Mary Trembles empty-handed from her door and was taken ill in consequence. They believed that women could become invisible and enter and leave rooms unknown to the victims. In an earlier trial Lydia Burman claimed that *Temperance had appeared unto her in the shape of a red pig*. This evidence too was accepted: in cases of witchcraft anything was credible.

One perplexing question is raised by the witches' apparent willingness to admit to all the accusations made against them. They made little or no attempt at denial or refutation of even the most fanciful of the accusations. It is possible, as Sir Francis North thought, that they were weary of their lives, and knowing that they had nothing to look forward to except to be outcasts and in the greatest poverty, submitted to the proceedings as a form of legalised suicide. Temperance Lloyd denied practising image magic, whilst assenting to all the other wild claims that can have had no foundation in reality whatsoever.

The general beliefs about the nature of witchcraft are well recorded in the literature of the time, though it is important to maintain the distinction between the beliefs of the common people, connected with folklore, and the pseudoscientific writings which influenced the beliefs of the authorities. The codification of witchcraft beliefs had found its first expression in a papal bull of 1484, which was expanded in the famous and influential book *Malleus Maleficarum* printed in 1486 and which formally established the intellectual and religious framework for the interpretation of the nature of witchcraft.

Well-organised, impassioned, and enjoying papal approval, the Malleus became one of the most influential of all early printed books... the Malleus declared that the four essential points of witchcraft were: renunciation of the Catholic faith, devotion of the body and soul to the service of evil, offering up unbaptised children to the Devil, and engaging in orgies that included intercourse with the Devil. In addition, witches typically shifted their shapes, flew through the air, abused the Christian sacraments, and confected magical ointments.[56]

These beliefs were adopted by Protestantism during the course of the Reformation. That period of religious strife co-incided with the European witch craze in which so many thousands of harmless old women were killed.

The traditional English view of witchcraft was of people who caused various misfortunes, or *maleficia*, which could not be easily attributed to natural causes or ascribed to God. Continental ideas about witchcraft were slow to reach England, and did not become widespread until the reign of James I. 'After his marriage in 1589 his life was threatened by a group of witches motivated by political ends and they were burned to death as both traitors and witches. He became utterly convinced of the reality of witches after this incident and wrote a book on the subject entitled Dæmonologie in 1597 which became the text book for future witch hunters.'[57] His ideas came with him to England, and under his influence a new statute against witchcraft was passed in 1604, and this established for the first time in law the concepts of diabolical pacts and worship and other continental ideas which were quickly taken up and applied during the witch craze of the 1640s, especially by such people as Matthew Hopkins, self-styled Witch Finder General, who used the book as his *vade mecum*.

English witches were believed to have 'caused diseases and fits, harmed livestock, hurt infants and small children, and kept familiars.'[58] Familiars were demons who accompanied witches, often in the form of animals, such as the witch's cat, but also dogs, toads and a whole menagerie of other real and imaginary creatures.

What to modern eyes seems the irrationality of these beliefs has to be set against the background of a rapidly changing society, where the traditional, medieval world was giving way to modern, industrial society, with all the tensions that this engendered. It was in these conditions that 'the insecurities and terrors of society were projected upon certain individuals who could then be tortured, killed and so removed.'[59]

The introduction to the pamphlet *A True and Impartial Relation of the Informations against Three Witches...* makes clear what were the sources of the beliefs of the educated classes and the authorities at that time. Although its authorship is not stated, it 'was written by a faithful and able hand employed in taking the examinations and confessions'. This author in his introduction encouraged the doubter of witchcraft to 'study the ancient writ' and the laws of England, from King Alfred to King James. He ended with the exhortation: 'Thou mayest at leisure consult the learned monarch King James in his *Dæmonologia*, fol. 91 and the late trial of witches before the honourable judicious great man, Judge Hales. See also Dr More's *Saducismus Triumphatus*, where the subject of witches and spirits is handled at large.'

His references make clear the precise influence of contemporary witchcraft literature. The 'late trial' refers to the pamphlet *A Tryal of Witches at the Assizes held at Bury St Edmonds for the County of Suffolk on the Tenth day of March, 1664, before Sir Matthew Hale, Kt...* which was published, significantly, in 1682, eighteen years after it had taken place.[60] The account does not have many obvious similarities with the Bideford pamphlet, beyond the usual accusation of secret teats, but its late publication gives an indication of the revival of interest in witchcraft in the 1680s.

Saducismus Triumphatus was the work not of Henry More, but of Joseph Glanvill, a native of Plymouth, fellow of the Royal Society, chaplain-in-ordinary to Charles II, and rector of Bath Abbey. It was first published in 1666 under the title *Philosophical Considerations Touching Witches and Witchcraft*. It ran into several editions, the fourth in 1668 being called *A Blow at Modern Saducism*. Glanvill died at Bath on 4 November 1680 and the work was republished posthumously the following year as *Saducismus Triumphatus*, with the addition of Henry More's *True Notion of a Spirit*, a translation of his work *Enchiridion Metaphysicum*. His friend Henry More was a member of the group known as the Cambridge Platonists, who attempted to reconcile religion and science. More's essay was an argument for the existence of the spirit, which he sought to support by the testimony of apparitions and witchcraft. Glanvill similarly called upon belief in the supernatural to defend religion by demonstrating the reality of Satan, namely that 'witchcraft furnished the only available contemporary evidence of a tangible kind for the existence of supernatural activity.'[61] In Glanvill's words: 'Atheism is begun in Saducism: and those that dare not bluntly say, There is no God, content themselves (for a fair step and introduction) to deny that there are spirits and witches.' Glanvill arranged his work firstly as a series of answers to objections, following this with what he perceived to be the attributes of witches, which were:

(1) their flying out of windows, after they have anointed themselves, to remote places

(2) their transformation into cats, hares and other creatures

(3) their feeling all the hurts in their own bodies which they have received in those

(4) their raising tempests by muttering some nonsensical words or performing ceremonies alike impertinent and ridiculous And

(5) their being sucked in a certain private place in their bodies by a familiar.[62]

None of this of course was new, but it provided a useful compendium of information of the sort that might have been read in Bideford, and new emphases.

The second part of the book consisted of accounts of witchcraft trials similar to those of Bideford, commencing with the discoveries of Robert Hunt, a Somerset justice, in the 1650s and 60s. These accounts were prefaced in the 1681 edition by an engraving illustrating some of the attributes listed by Glanvill, which very likely provided the inspiration for many of the charges made in Bideford. The Somerset cases printed by Glanvill resemble the later evidence from Bideford on several counts. On the first page it is described, for example, how the witness's daughter

had been more tormented than formerly and that though held in a chair by four or five people, sometimes six, by the arms, legs and shoulders, she would rise out of her chair and raise her body about three or four feet high. And that after, in her fits, she would have holes made in her hand, wrist, face and neck, and other parts of her body which they conceived to be with thorns.[63]

These were similar symptoms to those suffered by Grace Barnes in Bideford, as was the fact that 'her stomach seemed to swell.' The witch who was accused of causing the illness confessed 'that the devil about ten years since appeared to her in the shape of a handsome man, and after of a black dog; that he promised her money, and that she should live gallantly, and have the pleasure of the world for twelve years' and that she and other women 'met about nine of the clock in the night in the common near Trister Gate, where they met a man in black clothes with a little band to whom they did courtesy and due observance.' The idea of a coven of witches was fairly new to England, and the Somerset case was the first reported. The idea was also adopted in Bideford and the women there were also believed to be members of a coven, led by Temperance Lloyd. The many parallels between the two cases are sufficient to support this connection between them.

Chapter 4
The Symptoms

The three women who claimed to be bewitched all experienced the same symptoms which they and other witnesses described in detail. Grace Thomas's illness dated back eighteen months, to Candlemas 1681. In her statement she said that *on or about the second day of February 1681 she was taken with great pain in her head and all her limbs, which continued on her till near or upon the first day of August then following, and then her pains began to abate, and she was able to walk abroad to take the air, but in the night season she was in much pain, and not able to take her rest.* The pains returned with renewed vigour after her encounter with Temperance Lloyd on 1 June 1682: *In that very night she was taken very ill with sticking and pricking pains, as though pins and awls had been thrust into her body, from the crown of her head to the soles of her feet, and she lay as though it had been upon a rack.* She had a similarly violent attack on 30 June, two days before she appeared before the justices to make a statement, when *she was again pinched and pricked to the heart, with such cruel thrusting pains in her head, shoulders, arms, hands, thighs and legs, as though the flesh would have been then immediately torn from the bones with a man's fingers and thumbs.*

Grace Barnes did not make her statement until a month later, when she recalled the start of her affliction in similar terms: *about the middle of the month of May last past she was taken with very great pains of sticking and pricking in her arms, breast, and heart, as though divers awls had been pricked or stuck into her body, and was in great tormenting pain for many days and nights together, with a very little intermission.*

Her husband John had made his statement a fortnight earlier with similar details: *his wife was taken with very great pains of sticking and pricking in her arms, stomach and breast as though she had been stabbed with awls being so described unto him by her in such a manner as he though that she would have died immediately, and in such sad condition she hath continued unto this present day, in tormenting and grievous pains.* Her latest attack had occurred that weekend, a week after Temperance Lloyd had been imprisoned. That Sunday morning *his wife was again taken worse than before, insomuch as four men and women could hardly hold her.*

Dorcas Coleman, the third victim, claimed to be the longest suffering. Since August 1680 *she was taken in tormenting pains, by pricking in her arms, stomach and heart, in such a manner as she was never taken so before... She hath continued so ever since more or less every week.*

Other symptoms were also described. There were the nine pricks in Grace Thomas's knee, her claim that *she was even plucked out over her bed and lay in this condition for the space of three hours, and how, on 1 June, she was bound and seemingly chained up with all her sticking pains gathered together in her belly, so that on a sudden her belly was swollen as big as two bellies which caused her to cry out, 'I shall die! I shall die!' and in this sad condition she lay as though she had been dead for a long space (which those persons that were in the chamber with her did compute to be about two hours).*

Similar symptoms were recorded in earlier witchcraft trials, including the Somerset cases of 1660, and were also observed in the Salem witch trials in New England ten years later. The detailed accounts of the 1692 Salem trials describe convulsive fits, temporary loss of hearing, speech, sight and memory, choking sensations, loss of appetite, hallucinations and the sensation of being pinched and bitten, including actual marks on the skin.[64] Dorcas Coleman's husband reported just such strange happenings: *about three months now last past his wife was sitting in a chair and being speechless, he did see Susanna Edwards to come into the chamber under a pretence to visit her, whereupon his wife did strive to come at her but could not get out of the chair. Upon which he and Thomas Bremincom did endeavour to help her out of the chair, and Susanna did go towards the chamber door, and that when Susanna was come at the chamber door, she Dorcas (remaining speechless as aforesaid) did slide out of the chair upon her back, and so strove to come at her, but was not able to rise from the ground, until Susanna was gone down the stairs.* Dorcas Coleman and Thomas Bremincom repeated the story, he adding the detail that *she could neither see nor speak, by reason that her pains were so violent upon her.*

What the victims' illnesses have in common is their long, drawn out nature. In an analysis of over 1,200 witchcraft cases in Essex in the period 1550-1700 it has been pointed out that 'those whose deaths were ascribed to witches characteristically languished some time before they died.'[65] This, and the vivid descriptions provided by the witnesses and victims, tie in with the then popular belief in image magic.

This ancient and deadly form of magic provided a simple method of killing a man, and one that was comparatively safe, since the image-maker did not need to approach his dying victim, and with any luck at all could probably avoid incurring suspicion. A figure roughly resembling the person destined to die was secretly made of clay or wax, or sometimes, of wood. It was given the victim's name, because his name was supposed to be an integral part of its owner's personality. Often a strand of his hair, or some nail-parings, or shreds of his clothing were added to the effigy, to give it greater power. It was pierced with nails or pins and thorns, and either melted slowly before a fire, or buried in the earth… In all the parts where the nails or pins were driven, he suffered piercing torments in the corresponding parts of his body… Where an effigy was buried, or drowned, death was slow; as the image gradually mouldered in earth or water, so its original declined and withered, and finally died of some painful wasting disease.[66]

Grace Thomas in fact died four years later: she was buried on 23 March 1686. It is therefore reasonable to presume that she was genuinely ill; Thomas Eastchurch, her brother-in-law, *did repair unto several physicians, but she could never receive any benefit prescribed by them.* Nevertheless, her symptoms were those of an hysterical attack, in the strictly medical sense of the term. At that time, though, the next step, to remedy the complaint, was 'hunting down the witch and countering her magic, occupations which both took the mind off the grief and held out a partial hope of recovery.'[67]

Dorcas Coleman's husband was often away at sea, which may explain some of his wife's distressed behaviour. When she was examined by Dr Beare *upon view of her body he did say that it was past his skill to ease her of her pains; for he told her that she was bewitched.* The doctor was not alone of his profession at that time to evade the possibility of failure by blaming witchcraft. His patient was only too glad to seize this opportunity of explaining her illness, and the cause was quickly found in the person of Susanna Edwards.

Sir Francis North, Lord Guilford, Lord Chief Justice of the Common Pleas: frontispiece to Roger North's Life of the Right Honourable Francis North... *(1742)*

Chapter 5
The Trial at Exeter Assizes

The Machinery of Justice

Temperance Lloyd had been committed to Exeter Gaol on Saturday 8 July 1682, and Susanna Edwards and Mary Trembles had followed her there on Tuesday 19 July, and there all three awaited their trial. The principal criminal courts at that time were the assizes which took place twice a year, during Lent and during the summer. Assizes were not permanent institutions, nor were they in permanent session, but judges of the higher courts in London were appointed specifically on each occasion that the assizes were held. The country was divided into six 'circuits' and the two judges travelled to each of the principal towns of each circuit. Devon lay in the Western circuit, comprising the counties of Cornwall, Devon, Dorset, Somerset, Hampshire and Wiltshire. The two judges dealt with both civil and criminal cases, the latter chiefly consisting of 'murder, robbery, burglary and grand larceny, together with other serious offences such as rape, coining and witchcraft.'[68] One of their chief functions was the performance of a gaol delivery: the trying of all persons committed to the gaols by the justices on suspicion of having committed a felony. It was quite by chance that, only a month after the witches' committal to Exeter Gaol, the two judges reached Exeter on the next stage of the summer circuit.

The Judges

The trial took place at the Exeter assizes held at Exeter Castle on Monday 14 August 1682. By that time the whole of Exeter was excited by the affair, curiosity aroused by the three unfortunate old women who 'were hurried out of the country to be tried at Exeter for witchcraft; and the city rang with tales of their preternatural exploits.'[69] In an account of the trial Roger North described how

> The women were very old, decrepit, and impotent, and were brought to the assizes with as much noise and fury of the rabble against them as could be shewed on any occasion. The stories of their acts were in everyone's mouth, and they were not content to belie them in the country, but even in the city where they were to be tried miracles were fathered upon them, as that the judges' coach was fixed upon the castle bridge, and the like. All which the country believed, and accordingly persecuted the wretched old creatures. A less zeal in a city or kingdom hath been the overture of defection and revolution, and if these women had been acquitted, it was thought the country people would have committed some disorder.[70]

The two judges appointed for the assizes held that summer in Exeter were Sir Francis North, (later created Lord Guilford) the Lord Chief Justice of the Common Pleas, together with Sir Thomas Raymond, of the King's Bench. North had strong personal feelings against trials for witchcraft. According to Roger North, his brother and biographer, who was with him at Exeter, he 'dreaded the trying of a witch.' He had already been involved in a witchcraft trial a year or two previously when his scepticism led to an acquittal. On this occasion 'it fell out that Raymond sat on the Crown side there, which freed his lordship of the care of such trials. But he had really a concern upon him at what happened; which was, that his brother [i.e. colleague] Raymond's passive behaviour should let those poor women die.'[71] By that time, though, North was a sick man, and only too glad that he had civil cases to deal with, leaving Raymond to deal with the criminal cases.

Indictments

From the list of prisoners in gaol the clerks of the court prepared a calendar, or list, of all the prisoners to be tried together with the names of all the people who were making the charges and all those who would be required to give evidence. In this case, it would be the people who had made statements to the Bideford justices. From this the clerks then drew up bills of indictment. Then the grand jury which had been appointed, consisting of the more substantial freeholders of the county, was sworn and its members went through the bills of indictment with the accusers and witnesses who had come down from Bideford in a run-through of the trial. From this the grand jury decided if there was a prima facie case. This meeting took place in secrecy, in order to protect the accusers if the case was rejected. This was what happened in the case of two other Bideford women who were accused of witchcraft that same summer. On 21 July 1682 a record was made in the Bideford Sessions book of:

> Mr Mayor's letter to Mr Hill the town clerk concerning Mary Beare and Elizabeth Caddy with several informations against them. Against Mary Beare there was no prosecution, but against Elizabeth Caddy (who was out upon bail) there was an indictment preferred by Mary Weekes, the wife of Robert Weekes of Bideford, and by the grand jury returned with an *ignoramus*.[72]

The justices dealt with this case quite differently to the first, though they followed the same, correct procedures. The mayor decided not to allow any proceedings against Mary Beare and refused to issue a warrant for her arrest. Mary Weekes was presumably more forceful, and insisted on charges being pressed against Elizabeth Caddy who was, however, released on bail by the mayor and his fellow justice. Their lack of support for the prosecution no doubt led to its rejection by the grand jury when it was considered along with all the other cases before the assizes. Possibly these women were of higher social standing, or perhaps the justices were increasingly afraid of the witch hunt getting out of hand.

The Trial

The next stage took place in the courtroom, after the indictments had been 'found', or approved, by the grand jury, and was the arraignment of the prisoners. They were called to the bar and the first defendant would be told by the clerk of the court: 'Temperance Lloyd, hold up thy hand.' This was to ensure that the correct prisoner was being tried. Then the clerk read out the indictment in English: 'Thou art here indicted by the name of Temperance Lloyd, late of Bideford, widow, for that thou didst bewitch Lydia Burman unto death and that thou didst by witchcraft consume the body of Grace Thomas.' The clerk then asked: 'How sayest thou, Temperance Lloyd, art thou guilty of this felony as it is laid in the indictment whereof thou standest indicted or not guilty?'[73] According to one account of the trial, 'Temperance Lloyd who was the eldest of the three, pleaded to her indictment and owned the accusation.'[pdf] According to the official record of the trial, however, all three pleaded not guilty, possibly at the behest of the judge acting in their interest.[75] The other two women followed Temperance Lloyd and underwent the same procedure, Susanna Edwards being indicted for bewitching Dorcas Coleman and Mary Trembles for bewitching Grace Barnes. This was not strictly accurate, but the reasons for it are made clear in a memorandum in the Bideford Sessions book:

> Susanna Edwards and Mary Trembles having severally confessed upon their examinations that they had bewitched Grace Barnes they could not be indicted for the same crimes severally, wherefore Mary Trembles was indicted only for practising witchcraft upon Grace Barnes and Susanna was severally indicted for practising witchcraft upon the body of Dorcas Coleman.[76]

Once the prisoners had been arraigned, the petty jury was impanelled to hear the evidence and give a verdict. Each of the witnesses then gave evidence on oath. In this trial their written statements made in Bideford were read out. Hearsay was still generally accepted as evidence at that time, particularly so in a trial for witchcraft:

> Witchcraft, because of its secret and almost unprovable nature, was considered a crime apart. For this reason the normal rules of evidence and trial were modified. Suspicion alone was sufficient grounds for accusation; it was proper to use children as witnesses; absence from the scene of the crime was no alibi; the victim's character and events occurring many years before and not in the least related to the particular crime were relevant. The 'sufficient proofs', any one of which was strong enough to lead to a conviction for witchcraft, were as follows: accusation by another 'witch'; an unnatural mark on the body of the accused, supposedly caused by the Devil or a familiar; two witnesses to the pact with the Devil or who had seen the accused entertain the small familiars sent by him. One leading contemporary authority, for example, argued that if a person gave a child an apple and the child soon afterwards became ill, as long as there was known malice between them, this was proof enough to be grounds for execution. One of the strongest proofs was the confession of the accused, or a cross-accusation by another proven witch.[77]

The same criteria apply equally well in the trial of the Bideford witches, in almost every detail. In her final questioning, for example,

Temperance Lloyd was asked if *she did bewitch the children*. She replied: *I sold apples, and the child took the apple from me, and the mother took the apple from the child, for which I was very angry; but the child died of the smallpox.*

In addition to the evidence presented against them the accused also spoke to the court, freely confessing their crimes. The judge then asked the jury for their verdict, and in the circumstances of an emotional situation and a weak judge, the verdict of guilty on all charges was no surprise. Roger North was critical of Judge Raymond:

> The judge made no nice distinctions, as to how possible it was for old women in a sort of melancholy madness, by often thinking in pain, and want of spirits, to contract an opinion of themselves that was false; and that their confession ought not to be taken against themselves, without a plain evidence that it was rational and sensible, no more than that of a lunatic, or distracted person; but he left the point upon the evidence fairly (as they call it) to the jury, and they convicted them.[78]

Lord North wrote an account of the trial the following day to Sir Leoline Jenkins, the Secretary of State:

> Here have been three old women condemned for witchcraft; your curiosity will make you enquire of the circumstances. I shall only tell you that what I had from my brother [i.e. colleague] Raymond, before whom they were tried, that they were the most old, decrepit, despicable, miserable creatures that ever he saw. A painter would have chosen them out of the whole country for figures of that kind to have drawn by.
>
> The evidence against them was very full and fanciful, but their own confessions exceeded it. They appeared not only weary of their lives, but to have a great deal of skill to convict themselves. Their description of the sucking devils with saucer-eyes was as natural that the jury could not choose but believe them.'[79]

Lord North's personal feelings about the trial are made clear by his brother Roger North who tells how he was

> never more puzzled than when a popular cry was at the heels of a business, for then he had his jury to deal with, and if he did not tread upon eggs, they would conclude sinistrously, and be apt to find against his opinion. And, for this reason, he dreaded the trying of a witch. It is seldom that a poor wretch is brought to trial upon that account, but there is, at the heels of her, a popular rage that does little less than demand her to be put to death; and, if a judge is so clear and open as to declare against that impious vulgar opinion, that the devil himself has

power to torment and kill innocent children, or that he is pleased to divert himself with the good people's cheese, butter, pigs, and geese, and the like errors of the ignorant and foolish rabble, the countrymen (the triers) cry, this judge hath no religion, for he doth not believe in witches; and so, to show they have some, hang the poor wretches. All which tendency to mistake requires a very prudent and moderate carriage in a judge, whereby to convince, rather by detecting of the fraud, than by denying authoritatively such power to be given to old women.[80]

Roger North is a little unfair to the 'foolish rabble': the clergy and justices of Bideford share some of the blame. Lord North evaded responsibility for the trial, leaving it to Sir Thomas Raymond, 'a mild passive man, who had neither dexterity nor spirit to oppose a popular rage'.[81] Perhaps Roger North was anxious to exonerate his brother. Another version survived, now lost, but fortunately quoted by a later writer:

There is indeed some evidence that Raymond wished not to condemn the women, but yielded nevertheless to public opinion. In a pamphlet published five years later it is stated that the judge

in his charge to the jury gave his opinion that these three poor Women (as he supposed) were weary of their Lives, and that he thought it proper for them to be carried to the Parish from whence they came, and that the Parish should be charged with their Maintenance; for he thought their oppressing Poverty had constrained them to wish for Death.' Unhappily the neighbours made such an outcry that the women were found guilty and sentenced.

This is from a later and somewhat untrustworthy account, but it fits in well with what North says of the case.[82]

The three women themselves made the manipulation of such a trial in their favour impossible, with their lurid confessions. One account describes how

the old one confessed plainly that she had caused several ships at sea to be cast away... she confessed also that the devil lay carnally with her for nine nights together... this old witch was without doubt perfectly resolute, not minding what should become of her immortal soul, but rather impudently at, as well as after, her trial, so audacious, that she had done so many wicked exploits.[83]

Roger North had a clearer perception of what was really taking place, giving a pathetic portrait of the women who 'as to sense or understanding, were scarce alive; but were overwhelmed with melancholy, and waking dreams, and so stupid as no one could suppose they knew either the construction or consequence of what they said.' He also dismissed the statements taken by the justices in Bideford:

All the rest of the evidence was trifling. I, sitting in the court the next day, took up the file of informations, taken by the justices, which were laid out upon the table, and against one of the old women, read thus: 'This informant saith he saw a cat leap in at her (the old woman's) window when it was twilight; and this informant farther saith, that he verily believeth the said cat to be the devil, and more saith not.'[84]

There is no such statement surviving in the evidence, though it appears to be drawn from the statements of Thomas Eastchurch and Anne Wakely, and it captures well the flavour of the original.

305.—Rougemont Castle.

The entrance to Rougemont Castle, Exeter (1845)

Sir Thomas Raymond, judge of the King's Bench
[Royal Courts of Justice]

Chapter 6
The Execution

Although condemned to be hanged, there was the possibility in the circumstances of a reprieve, as was to happen in some subsequent witchcraft trials. On this occasion, however, Lord North advised against such a measure when he wrote to Sir Leoline Jenkins who, as Secretary of State, possessed the power to authorise a reprieve.

> Sir, I find the country so fully possessed against them that although some of the virtuosi may think these the effects of confederacy, melancholy, or delusion, and that young folks are altogether as quick-sighted as they who are old and infirm; yet we cannot reprieve them without appearing to deny the very being of witches, which, as it is contrary to law, so I think it would be ill for his Majesty's service, for it may give the faction occasion to set afoot the old trade of witchfinding that may cost many innocent persons their lives, which the justice will not prevent.[85]

This was the political background to, and the real reason for, their eventual deaths: the fear of a popular uprising against an unpopular verdict, and the more important fear of providing ammunition for the 'faction', as had happened during the unhappy period of the trials of the Popish Plot three years previously, when many people lost their lives on the flimsiest of perjured evidence provided by the disreputable Titus Oates, a period which brought the whole judiciary into shameful disrepute. The 'faction' was also known as the Country Party, and was later to become known as the Whigs, and was responsible for manipulating these travesties of justice for its political ends. The deaths of the three women were seen as being justified by the avoidance of a greater evil.

Exeter Castle where the witches were tried: from Braun and Hoghenbeg's Civitates Orbis Terrarum *(1618)*

Having been sentenced to be hanged, the three women were returned to Exeter Gaol to await their executions, which took place on Friday 25 August 1682 before a large crowd at Heavitree outside Exeter. Mr Hann, the clergyman who believed himself to have been one of their victims after visiting Bideford, spoke to them concerning their crimes, which they mostly denied, the immediacy of their impending deaths giving them back their reason too late. Their last words were recorded as fully as could be taken in a case liable to so much noise and confusion. They denied all the charges of witchcraft: diabolical intercourse and pact, giving blood or possession of secret teats, when asked about them by Mr Hann. Mr Hann then prayed, after which Susanna Edwards requested that they sing part of the fortieth psalm together, an appropriate choice in the circumstances:

Withhold not thou thy tender mercies from me, O Lord: let thy lovingkindness and thy truth continually preserve me.

For innumerable evils have compassed me about: mine iniquities have taken hold upon me, so I am not able to look, they are more than the hairs of mine head: therefore my heart faileth me.

Be pleased, O Lord, to deliver me; O Lord, make haste to help me.

Susanna Edwards was the first to be executed. *As she mounted the ladder, she said, 'The Lord Jesus speed me; though my sins be as red as scarlet the Lord Jesus can make them white as snow.' Then was executed.* Mary Trembles 'was very obstinate, and would not go, but lay down, insomuch that they were forced to tie her upon a horseback, for she was very loath to receive her deserved doom.' She had managed to compose herself by the time her turn for execution came, and said, standing before the gallows, *'Lord Jesus receive my soul, Lord Jesus speed me.,' and then also was executed.*

The hanging of Temperance Lloyd, reputed leader of the coven and cause of the others' corruption, came last. 'It is certainly affirmed the old witch… went all the way eating, and was seemingly unconcerned.'[86] She appears to have recovered her wits before execution. After praying with Mr Hann, and the other two had been hanged, she said *'Jesus Christ speed me well; Lord forgive all my sins; Lord Jesus Christ be merciful to my poor soul.'* At this point the sheriff for the county, who was in attendance, interjected and said to her *'You are looked on as the woman that had debauched the other two.'* He then proceeded to question her:

Sheriff Did you ever lie with devils?
Temperance No.
Sheriff Did you know of their coming to gaol?
Temperance No.
Sheriff Have you anything to say to satisfy the world?
Temperance I forgive them, as I desire the Lord Jesus Christ will forgive me. The greatest thing I did was to Mistress Grace Thomas, and I desire I may be sensible of it, and that the Lord Jesus Christ may forgive me. The devil met me in the street and bid me kill her and because I would not he beat me about the head and back.
Sheriff In what shape or colour was he?
Temperance In black, like a bullock.
Sheriff How do you know you did it? How went you in, through the keyhole or the door?
Temperance At the door.

47

Sheriff Had you no discourse with the devil?

Temperance Never but this day six weeks.

Sheriff You were charged about twelve years since, and did you never see the devil but this time?

Temperance Yes, once before. I was going for brooms, and he came to me and said, 'This poor woman has a great burden', and would help ease me of my burden; and I said, 'The Lord had enabled me to carry it so far, and I hope I shall be able to carry it further.'

Sheriff Did the devil never promise you anything?

Temperance No, never.

Sheriff Then you have served a very bad master, who gave you nothing. Well, consider you are just departing this world: do you believe there is a God?

Temperance Yes.

Sheriff Do you believe in Jesus Christ?

Temperance Yes, and I pray Jesus Christ to pardon all my sins.

And so was executed.

Witches being hanged, from Ralph Gardiner's England's Grievance Discovered in relation to the Coal Trade *(1655)*

Chapter 7
Aftermath

Temperance Lloyd, Mary Trembles and Susanna Edwards paid with their lives for the suspicion of witchcraft; Mary Beare and Elizabeth Caddy were more fortunate and never experienced imprisonment or judgement. They were not the last on whom the finger of suspicion fell: in 1686 'several informations against Abigail the wife of Robert Handford concerning the suspicion of witchcraft' were filed by the town clerk.[87] There is no further record of the case; presumably the charge was dropped.

Watkins, writing a century later, commented in relation to the trial that 'the belief of witchcraft remained very general in the town and neighbourhood, and there was always some poor devil, either on account of an unlucky visage, sour temper, or wretched poverty, set up as the object of terror and universal hatred, till about twenty years since.'[88] He was optimistic in his belief that witchcraft had died in Bideford, for Granville in his 'History of Bideford' recorded an early nineteenth-century case:

At this time also the popular belief in witchcraft was very strong, and, as an instance, one of the many stories, the truth of which was considered beyond doubt, may be given. An old woman named Molly Bryant, who lived in one of the old almshouses in Meddon Street, had the reputation of being able to turn herself at will into a hare. It was honestly thought that the old woman really availed herself of this power and often deceived the huntsmen, leading them a fine chase to no purpose. This caused a private of the regiment above mentioned [29th Foot Regiment] to vow vengeance on the old woman. He watched the house and one day 'saw a hare spying out of the keyhole.' He fired and hit the animal, which thereupon disappeared. On search being made Molly Bryant was found within her house, but it was noticed that she had suddenly become lame, and to the day of her death it was believed that the soldier had shot her when she was in the form of a hare and in the act of jumping through the keyhole.'[89]

There are many versions of this tale in the west country, starting with the trial of Julian Cox at Taunton in 1663. They all include the element of shape-shifting, and also the feeling of an injury by the witch which had been inflicted on the hare.

The memory of the 1682 lingered on in Bideford long afterwards. Tradition said that the three witches lived in a thatched cottage in Old Town which was burnt down in 1894, though a photograph of it survives.[90] A further reference to it in local folklore is quoted by W. H. Rogers in his unpublished history of Bideford written in 1939, from an unidentified guidebook of 'over thirty years ago.'

A mariner of Honestone Lane... declared... he had seen these three friendless old women meet on many occasions in the Parsonage Close at midnight 'mixing something in a crock'. He had also seen a little black man come out of the rectory; he had something like a spiked tail and a cloven foot. He went and gave something to the three old women, which they put into the crock. He then put his hand into a bag that he carried by his side and took out something bright which he handed to each of the crones. The little black man then disappeared among the trees by the rectory... he recognised the cracked voice of Susan Edwards say 'Thrice the brindled cat hath mewed,' which was followed by a wild burst of laughter, and then all three chanted in chorus,

'Beat the water, Trembles's daughter

Till the tempest gather o'er us;

Till the thunder strike with wonder,

And the lightning flash before us!

Beat the water, Trembles's daughter,

Ruin seize our foes, and slaughter!'

Whereupon he stood, he said, like one riveted to the spot at the sight of the wild orgy.'[91]

Although much influenced by Shakespeare, the ancient mariner obviously had a reasonably accurate knowledge of the events, including their location and the names of two of the women.

By the end of the seventeenth century witchcraft had passed from favour with intellectuals and was no longer accepted by the judges themselves. People no longer blamed witchcraft for their misfortunes, and this was reflected in the large increase in accusations of arson and other malicious injury. The last trial for witchcraft took place in 1712, and although found guilty and sentenced to death, the victim received a royal pardon. In 1736 the statute of 1604 was repealed, removing the legal penalties for witchcraft, though popular belief lingered on long after.

From Joseph Glanvill's Saducismus Triumphatus *(1681)*

51

References

1 A. L. Rouse *Sir Richard Grenville of the Revenge* (1937), 114.

2 Rouse, 233.

3 W. G. Hoskins *Bideford Gazette* , 31 December 1935.

4 W. G. Hoskins *Devon* (1954), 218.

5 W. H. Rogers *Notes on Bideford* (unpublished), II, 21.

6 . Watkins *An Essay towards the History of Bideford in the County of Devon* (1792), 126-31.

7 PRO PROB/11/313/folio 59

8 PRO PROB/11/335 1/folio 36

9 PRO PROB/11/384/folios 106

13 PRO PROB/11/407/folio 204

14 PRO PROB/11/417/folio 181

15 PRO PROB/11/417/folio 184

16 W. G. Hoskins *Devon* (1954), 218.

17 PRO PROB/11/413/folio 13

18 PRO PROB/11/413/folio 22

19 Bideford Parish Register.

20 PRO PROB/11/413/folio 21

21 Bideford Parish Register.

22 Bideford Parish Register and J. Barber *The Devon Historian,* 5 (1972), 31.

23 Sessions of the Peace Book for Bideford, 1659-1709 (DRO: 10640/S0 1).

24 *Report of the Commissioners concerning Charities (Devon)* (1826-32) II, 292-314.

25 Sessions Book.

26 H. Kamen *The Iron Century* (1976), 269.

27 Kamen, 268.

28 R. Granville *The History of Bideford* (1883), 77-8, quoting C. Mather, *Magnalia Christi Americana*, IV, 126 (pt i, §2), 1702. See also DNB sub Eaton, Nathaniel.

29 DNB sub Eaton, Nathaniel.

30 DRO: QS74/5/1-6.

31 Letters, John Hill to Francis Cooke (DRO: Basket A/2532).

32 DRO: QS74/5/734 R. Stanes (ed) *The Devon Historian*, 10 (1975),16.

35 Watkins, 129.

36 Letters, John Hill to Francis Cooke (DRO: Basket A//2613).

37 DRO: QS74/5/13.

38 Watkins, 48. See also, Inderwick *Side-Lights on the Stuarts*, p. 398.

39 J. Fox 'Memoirs' *TDA*, 29 (1897), 88

40 Sessions Book.

41 DRO

42

43 C. L'E. Ewen *Witchcraft and Demonianism* (1933), 441.

44 Sessions Book. See p. xx

45 J. H. Baker 'Criminal Courts and Procedure at Common Law 1550–1800' in J. S. Cockburn (ed) *Crime in England 1550–1800* (1977), 28.

46 Rogers, II, 68.

47 Baker, 32-3.

48 All quotations in italics are from *A True and Impartial Relation of the Information against Three Witches. . .* (1682).

49 A. Macfarlane *The Justice and the Mare's Ale* (1981), 26, quoting J. D. Marshall (ed.) *The Autobiography of William Stout of Lancaster, 1665-1752* (1967), 79.

50 *The Tryal, Condemnation, and Execution of Three Witches...*

51 J. B. Russell *A History of Witchcraft* (1980), 92.

52 C. Hansen *Witchcraft in Salem* (1969), 48.

53 Hansen

54 K. Thomas *Religion and the Decline of Magic* (1971), 679.

55 C. Larner *'Was witch hunting woman hunting?'* New Society 10 October 1981,11-12.

56 Russell, 79.

57 R. Holmes *The Legend of Sawny Beane* (1975), 89.

58 Russell, 92.

59 Russell, ?.

60 Ewen, 347.

61 B. Willey *The Seventeenth-Century Background* (1967),176.

62 J. Glanvill, *Saducismus Triumphatus* (1681), 6.

63 Glanvill, 69.

64 Hansen, 11.

65 A. Macfarlane

66 C. Hole *Witchcraft in England* (1977), 64-5..

67 Macfarlane,

68 Baker, 28.

69 R. North *The Life of the Right Honourable Francis North...* (1742), 19.

70 R. North *Examen*, quoted in Hole, 165.

71 R. North *The Life of the Right Honourable Francis North...* (1742), 19.

72 Sessions Book.

73 Baker, 33-4.

74 *The Tryal, Condemnation and Execution of Three Witches...* (1682), 2.

75 Ewen, 444.

76 Sessions Book.

77 Macfarlane, 78 North, Life, 1 92.

79 *Calendar of State Papers (Domestic) Charles II*, 348, quoted in Ewen, 372TDA, 6 (1874), 736-63, also in EHD 1660...

80 North, Life, 191.

81 R. North *Examen*, quoted in Hole, 165.

82 Wallace Notestein, *A History of Witchcraft in England from 1558* (1911).

83 *The Tryal, Condemnation...* , 4.

84 North, *Life*, 192.

85 See 79.

86 *The Tryal, Condemnation...* , 5-6.

87 Sessions Book.

88 Watkins, 267.

89 Grenville, 98.

90 M. Goaman *Old Bideford and District* (1978), 59.

91 Rogers, I, 85 note.

Appendices

Appendix One

Witchcraft discovered and punished.

OR, THE TRYALS AND CONDEMNATION OF THREE NOTORIOUS WITCHES,

Who were Tryed at the last Assizes, holden at the Castle of Exeter,

in the County of Devon: whereby they received Sentance for Death,

for bewitching several Persons, destroying Ships at Sea,

and Cattel by Lande, etc.

To the Tune of 'Doctor Faustus ' or 'Fortune my Foe '.

Now listen to my Song, good People all,

And I shall tell what lately did befall

At Exeter a place in Devonshire,

The like whereof of late you nere did hear.

At the last Assizes held at Exeter,

Three aged Women that Imprisoned were

For Witches, and that many had destroy'd;

Were thither brought in order to be try'd.

For Witchcraft, that Old Wicked Sin,

Which they for long time had continued in;

And joyn'd with Satan, to destroy the good

Sweet Innocents, and shed their harmless blood.

But now it most apparent does appear,
That they will now for such their deeds pay dear:
For Satan, having lull'd their Souls asleep,
Refuses Company with them to keep.

A known deceiver he long time has been,
To help poor Mortals into dangerous Sin;
Thereby to cut them off, that so they may
Be plung'd in Hell, and there be made his Prey.

So these Malicious Women at the last,
Having done mischiefs, were by Justice cast;
For it appear'd they Children had destroy'd,
Lamed Cattell, and the Aged much annoy'd,

Having Familiars always at their Beck,
Their Wicked Rage on Mortals for to wreck:
It being proved they used Wicked Charms,
To Murther Men, and bring about sad harms.

And that they had about their Body's strange
And Proper Tokens of their Wicked Change:
As Pledges that, to have their cruel will,
Their Souls they gave unto the Prince of Hell.

The Country round where they did live came in,
And all at once their sad complaints begin;
One lost a Child, the other lost a Kine,
This his brave Horses, that his hopeful Swine.

One had his Wife bewitch'd, the other his Friend,
Because in some things they the Witch offend:
For which they labour under cruel pain,
In vain seek remedy, but none can gain.

But Roar in cruel sort, and loudly cry
Destroy the Witch, and end our misery:
Some used Charms by Mountabanks set down,
Those cheating Quacks, that swarm in every Town.

But all's in vain, no rest at all they find,
For why? all Witches are to cruelty enclin'd;
And do delight to hear sad dying groans,
And such laments as wou'd pierce Marble Stones.

But now the Hand of Heaven has found them out,
And they to Justice must pay Lives, past doubt;
One of these Wicked Wretches did confess,
She Four Score Years of Age was, and no less.

And that she had deserved long before,
To be sent packing to the Stigian shore:
For the great mischiefs she so oft had done,
And wondered that her life so long had run.

She said the Devil came with her along,
Through Crouds of People, and bid her be strong:
And she no hand should have, but like a Lyer,
At the Prison Door he fled, and nere came nigh her.

The rest aloud, crav'd Mercy for their Sins
Or else the great deceiver her Souls gains;
For they have been lewd Livers many a day
And therefore did desire that all would Pray.

To God, to Pardon them, while thus they lie
Condemned for their Wicked Deeds to Die:
Which may each Christian do, that they may find
Rest for their Souls, though Wicked once inclin'd.

A traditional tune to the ballad 'Fortune My Foe'

Appendix Two

CALENDAR OF EVENTS

1658	Grace Ellyott of Bideford charged with witchcraft at Exeter Summer Assizes
1671	February 2 William Herbert accused Temperance Lloyd on his deathbed
March 14	Temperance accused of bewitching William Herbert
May 5	Temperance acquitted at Exeter Assizes
1672	
May 24	Death of Lydia Burman
1679	
May 15	Temperance accused of bewitching Anne Fellow
May 17	Accusation recorded at Bideford Sessions.
1680	
August	Susanna Edwards visits Dorcas Coleman who is taken ill
1681	
February 2	Grace Thomas's pains start
June 23	Grace Barnes complains against Peter Bagilhole
August 1	Grace Thomas's pains cease
Sept'r 26	Grace Thomas meets Temperance in street and taken ill
Sept'r 30	Cat goes into Thomas Eastchurch's house
1682	
April 18 (Easter Tuesday)	Grace Barnes in great pain
	Mary Trembles begs at Barnes's house
May 7	Disturbance at parish church
Thu June 1	Grace Thomas's belly swollen

Thu June 29	Anne Wakely sees magpie enter Grace Thomas's window
Fri June 30	Grace Thomas has bad pains
Sat July 1	Temperance Lloyd put in Bideford prison and Grace Thomas's pains cease
Sun July 2	Thomas Eastchurch questions Temperance Lloyd
	Temperance Lloyd searched for witch's mark
Mon July 3	Statements made against Temperance Lloyd
	Confession by Temperance Lloyd
Tue July 4	Temperance Lloyd questioned in church by Mr Ogilby
	Temperance Lloyd questioned by William Herbert
Sat July 8	Temperance Lloyd committed to gaol at Exeter
Mon July 17	William Edwards hears Susanna Edwards confess
Tue July 18	Susanna Edwards examined and confesses
	Statements made against Susanna Edwards
	Anthony Jones has fit
	Examination and confession of Mary Trembles
Wed July 19	Anthony Jones makes statement
	Susanna Edwards and Mary Trembles sent to Exeter gaol
Fri July 21	Mary Beare and Elizabeth Caddy accused by Mary Weekes
Wed July 26	Statements by John Coleman, Dorcas Coleman and Thomas Bremincom
Wed August 2	Statement by Grace Barnes
Sat August 12	Statement by William Herbert
Mon August 14	Trial at Exeter assizes
Tue August 15	Letter from Lord North to Secretary of State
Fri August 25	Execution at Heavitree

Appendix Three

SOME OF THE PRINCIPAL CHARACTERS

Humphrey Ackland appointed parish clerk of Bideford in 1637. Master of Lydia Burman.

Grace Barnes wife of John Barnes; victim of witchcraft.

George Beare doctor who attended Dorcas Coleman. His wife Elinor died 23 October 1666.

Thomas Bremincom (alias Brimacombe) Uncle of John Coleman.

Lydia Burman spinster and servant of Humphrey Ackland. She testified against Temperance Lloyd at her trial in 1671. Buried 24 May 1672, and her death was blamed on Temperance Lloyd.

Dorcas Coleman wife of John; claimed to be bewitched by Susanna Edwards.

John Coleman mariner; husband of Dorcas and nephew of Thomas Bremincom. Fined for attending Conventicle 31 May 1674, but there described as a taylor.

Jane Dallyn wife of Simon Dallyn, mariner, whom she married on 2 January 1656. Died 1674 from an eye infection which was blamed on Temperance Lloyd.

John Davie alderman and justice of the peace. Mayor in 1671, 1680 and 1687.

John Dunning gentleman reputedly from Great Torrington who questioned Temperance Lloyd in Bideford prison.

Elizabeth Eastchurch Wife of Thomas and sister of Grace Thomas. Fined for attending a Conventicle 31 May 1674. Daughter of Christopher Thomas, gentleman.

Susanna Edwards illegitimate daughter of Rachel Winslade. Christened 2 December 1612, married 9 October 1639 to David Edwards. A widow, accused of witchcraft, and hanged 25 August 1682.

William Edwards blacksmith. Fined for attending Conventicles on 31 May and 9 June 1674, but described as a potter.

Anne Fellow	daughter of Anne and Edward Fellow, a gauger of excise, alleged victim of Temperance Lloyd.
Cicely Galsworthy	matron who searched Temperance Lloyd for devil's mark (or witch's teat) in 1679 and 1682. Buried 6 November 1697.
Thomas Gist	mayor of Bideford 1681-82.
Mr Hann	clergyman who officiated with his son in the parish church in 1681, and believed himself bewitched by Temperance Lloyd. Visited the witches in gaol and attended them at their execution. A William Hann was born at Haslebury in Dorset, received his MA from Pembroke College, Oxford in 1648, becoming a fellow of New College, to be ejected in 1660.
John Hill	town clerk of Bideford, persecutor of the Nonconformists.
Honor Hooper	servant of Thomas Eastchurch. Searched Temperance Lloyd with Anne Wakely and others.
Anthony Jones	husbandman, husband of Joan and victim of Susanna Edwards.
Temperance Lloyd	widow. Accused of witchcraft.
Michael Ogilby	rector of Bideford from 1674 until his death in 1699. Rebuilt the rectory. Involved in many disputes with his parishioners.
Grace Thomas	sister of Elizabeth Eastchurch and alleged victim of Temperance Lloyd. Buried 23 March 1686.
Mary Trembles	spinster and friend of Susanna Edwards. Accused of witchcraft by Grace Barnes. Possibly daughter of Trojan Trembles, alias Trimell, who was buried in 1671.
Anne Wakely	wife of William, husbandman; neighbour and friend of the Eastchurches; nursed Grace Thomas; searched Temperance Lloyd for the devil's mark (or witch's teat).
Agnes Whitefield	née Gist, married John, a cordwainer, on 29 September 1656. She was in the Barnes's house when Grace accused Mary Trembles.

Appendix Four

PRIMARY PRINTED SOURCES

This account of the trial of the Bideford witches is based on the excellent contemporary sources which have survived. The most important of these is the pamphlet *A True and Impartial Relation of the Informations against Three Witches...* published in 1682 after their trial and execution. This is the printed version of the statements made by witnesses to the justices in Bideford before the trial. The originals were subsequently lost or destroyed, and we are fortunate that they have survived in this printed form. It is this pamphlet that has been widely reprinted. I have traced the following:

Boulton, R. *History of Magic* (1715) 2, 216-54.

Howell, T. T. *State Trials* (1816-1831) 8, col. 1017-40.

Watkins, J. *History of Bideford* (1792) 233-67.

TDA 6 (1874), 736-63.

Ewen, C. L'E. *Witchcraft and Demonianism* (1933), 367-72.

The pamphlet is given the reference number T2502 in Wing's catalogue. There are copies in several libraries, including the British Library, the Bodleian and the Westcountry Studies library in Exeter. There is a copy in Bideford library which unfortunately lacks the first two leaves bearing the title page and preface. The version in the 1883 reprint of Watkins is heavily bowdlerised.

The other pamphlet concerning the trial, *The Tryal Condemnation and Execution of Three Witches...* is much shorter and scarcer: only three copies are known to exist, one in Bideford library and the other two in the British Library. It also appears to be unreliable in its content.

Wallace Notestein in his book A History of Witchcraft in England 1558–1718 (1911) quotes from a third pamphlet: *The Life and Conversation of Temperance Floyd, Mary Lloyd and Susannah Edwards... ; Lately Condemned at Exeter Assizes; together with a full Account of their first Agreement with the Devil: with the manner how they prosecuted their devilish Sorceries...*, (London, 1687). This he describes as 'a later and somewhat untrustworthy account.' Antonia Fraser in *The Weaker Vessel* (19xx) quotes from these pamphlets, using Notestein as her main source of information.

Two broadside ballads are associated with the trial. *Witchcraft Discovered and Punished* was described and inaccurately quoted by Baring-Gould.* It is listed in Wing as W3138 which ascribes a unique copy incorrectly to the British Library. Although no original can at present be traced, there appear to have been two versions printed. One was used by J. Ashton in his *Century of Ballads* (1887) and is given in Appendix One. The other, printed in the *Roxburghe Ballads* (1966) has many minor variations of punctuation or spelling. Its woodcut illustration is also finer than that reproduced by Ashton.

The second broadside ballad was called *The Undutiful Daughter of Devonshire* (Wing U48). The version in the British Library, which is dated 1685-92, bears no obvious relevance to the Bideford trial, but a later American version of 1765 adds the information that this daughter was 'of Bideford, Devon, bore a child to Mr Lawrence of that place... hanged for murder after a confession of witchcraft' and a 'learned Dr H... y discovered her witchcraft'. Presumably the printer in Philadelphia combined song and story to improve its appeal, in much the same manner that the legend of Sawney Bean became the legend of the Clovelly cannibals. It is unfortunate that a copy of this version of the ballad cannot at present be traced.‡

* S. Baring-Gould, *Devonshire Characters and Strange Events*, (1908),2 74-7.

‡ *Notes and Queries*, 18 June 1932. 442

MANUSCRIPT SOURCES

PUBLIC RECORD OFFICE
Wills:
William Ernle PROB/11/311/folio 59
William Mill PROB/11/3 13/folio 41
William Greening PROB/11/335/folio 36
John Darracott PROB/11/342/folio 75
Richard Greening PROB/11/384/folios 106-107
Henry Amory PROB/11/391/folio 74
John Frost PROB/11/390/folio 14
Hartwell Buck PROB/11/407/folio 204
George Darracott PROB/11/417/folio 181
Abraham Gearing PROB/11/417/folio 184
Christopher Pollard PROB/11/413/folio 13
Thomas Conybeare PROB/11/413/folio 22
Mary Beard PROB/11/413/folio 21

DEVON RECORD OFFICE
Bideford Parish Church: Register of Baptisms, Marriages and Burials
Bideford Sessions of the Peace Book
Letters from John Hill.

Appendix Five

Glossary of Legal Terms

arraign indict before a tribunal

assize   periodical session for administration of justice.

circuit   twice-yearly journey of judge to hold court in main towns of a region

delivery   trial of prisoners held in gaol at assizes

deposition   evidence or allegation given under oath

felony   serious crime requiring trial at assizes

grand jury   freeholders appointed to inquire into indictment to see if sufficient evidence to merit a trial

ignoramus   dismissal of charge by grand jury

indictment   legal process by which formal accusation is presented to grand jury

maleficium   commission of evil deeds by witchcraft

mittimus   warrant to gaoler to receive and retain a prisoner until tried

petty jury   twelve persons appointed to find a verdict at assizes

recognizance   bond paid to court as security for a condition

severally   separately

Appendix Six

Abbreviations and Conventions

DRO Devon Record Office, Exeter

PRO Public Record Office, London

TDA Transactions of the Devonshire Association

DNB Dictionary of National Biography

Spelling, punctuation and capitalisation have been modernised in all the quotations. Place and personal names have been standardised and made to conform with modern usage, and dates are in new style, with the year starting on 1 January. Abbreviations have been expanded.

Since much of the material is in the form of legal depositions, where there is a good deal of repetition and redundant wording, the following alterations and omissions have been made: 'this Informant' is changed to 'he' or 'she'; 'said' and 'aforesaid' are omitted; 'of Bideford' is omitted where superfluous.

Quotations from the pamphlet *A True and Impartial Relation of the Informations against Three Witches...* are printed in italics.

Printed in Great Britain
by Amazon

10208583R00045